WISDOM TRILOGY

THE NOBLE RIVER

BOOK ONE
INNER BREATH

EDITOR
STEPHEN K. SIMS

Published by Stephen K. Sims
First edition, April 2021

Library and Archives Canada Cataloguing in Publication

Sims, Stephen, 1947–, editor
THE NOBLE RIVER wisdom trilogy

Issued in print and electronic formats.

ISBN numbers:
BOOK ONE
978-0-9940899-4-6 (paperback)
978-0-9940899-5-3 (e-book)

BOOK TWO
978-0-9940899-6-0 (paperback)
978-0-9940899-7-7 (e-book)

BOOK THREE
978-0-9940899-8-4 (paperback)
978-0-9940899-9-1 (e-book)

Art illustrations: Normand Laurin
Book production, outreach: Tristan Telak
Layout, cover design: Ted Sancton

For quantity sales, discounts are available,
contact: thenobleriver@gmail.com

Also published by the author:
River of Awareness (2009) / second edition (2021)
The Wisdom of Authenticity (2015)

For further information, please visit:
www.stephenksims.com

The following titles complete
the three-book collection:

BOOK TWO
MUD PATH

BOOK THREE
SOUL FIRE

DEDICATION

To all who seek to follow
noble purpose, an open path;
the way of visionary fire.

To all who seek to awaken
wonder and wisdom, soulfulness;
the way of deep imagination.

To all who seek to find
a still point, loving generosity;
the way of pure compassion.

TRILOGY OUTLINE

The River has secrets waiting to be told...

...a thousand voices of wisdom guiding a journey into love.

INNER BREATH
BOOK ONE

SETTING FORTH
1   wisdom
2   journey
3   call
4   longing / seeking
5   awakening
6   becoming
7   change
8   vision / potential
9   essence
10   meaning

THE RELENTLESS QUEST
11   self-development
12   body-mind healing
13   readiness / risk
14   courage
15   intention / purpose
16   inwardness
17   imagination
18   myth / symbol
19   thresholds
20   hero path

THE AWARENESS TREK
21   now-presence
22   self-awareness
23   attentiveness
24   questions
25   insight
26   action
27   repression
28   emotional literacy
29   authenticity
30   self-knowledge

MUD PATH
BOOK TWO

THE WAY IS LOST
31 non-consciousness
32 ignorance / limitation
33 darkness / evil
34 bias
35 narrow-mindedness
36 refusal / reluctance
37 denial / distraction
38 self-deception
39 suffering / pain
40 path of decline

NIGHT DESCENT
41 fear / anxiety
42 greed
43 anger / resentment
44 grief / sadness
45 depression / despair
46 loneliness
47 guilt
48 projection / blame
49 conflict / violence
50 attachment

MASKS OF TIME
51 complex psyche
52 ego-striving
53 persona
54 shadow
55 alienation
56 inauthenticity
57 ego deconstruction
58 transformation
59 impermanence
60 death

SOUL FIRE
BOOK THREE

INTER-BELONGING
61 self-affirmation
62 individuation
63 friendship
64 mentoring
65 interconnection
66 differentiation
67 dialogue
68 moral integrity
69 ethics
70 nature

THE NOBLE HEART
71 consciousness
72 happiness
73 generosity / gratitude
74 humility
75 non-attachment
76 forgiveness
77 non-violence
78 peace / justice
79 love
80 compassion

THE ETERNAL VOYAGE
81 spirituality / soul
82 religious meaning
83 the divine
84 meditation / prayer
85 stillness / solitude
86 transcendence
87 emergence
88 transfiguration
89 the infinite
90 oneness

TRILOGY PROLOGUE

*I didn't know that there is a place deep
inside where one's real life goes on,
much like an underground river
in parched, dry country, which flows
whether one knows about it or not.*

Sharon Butala

I have had a lifelong fascination with rivers. Perhaps it is no surprise that now, in the evening of life, I find myself with a dwelling place on the banks of a lively flow of waters. I never tire of gazing at the river on its bold journey into the unknown.

The question *where are you going?* seems to arise whenever I find myself in the presence of a river – drawing my awareness to 'a place deep inside' to 'an underground river' where my 'real life' waits to be found. This inner river holds a timeless mystery that summons higher possibility – each threshold of growth into my unrecognized self brings surprise, the unexpected, new possibility.

Outer purpose in one's life flows from a connection to one's inner depth – where meaning is revealed. As a river seeks out its destiny with steady determination, in like manner, the *river of life* leads us over countless thresholds of change, drawing forth new dimensions of consciousness that ignite the vital energies of life.

Wisdom teaches us laws of harmony and inspires courage: it invites us to form a resolute commitment to wholeness and wellness that marks out a way of noble purpose. When deep intention is combined with a practice of skillful attention, we attain a degree of river mastery to steady our journey of love.

On this epic adventure of self-discovery, there are secrets the *River* wishes to tell. Even as we seek wisdom, it is seeking us. May we be open to receive its instruction, and the blessings of a noble heart.

The Noble River wisdom trilogy gathers insights that have over a lifetime inspired my personal journey of self-discovery. A few drops from a vast ocean of knowledge, the voices within these pages mirror the infinite unknown which all of us are invited to explore, and out of which is born deep creativity and compassion.

Please note that none of the voices have been gender- corrected. Reprinted in their original articulation, they reflect the era in which they first found expression.

BOOK ONE
INNER BREATH

THE NOBLE RIVER wisdom trilogy guides us on an adventure of self-discovery. The *inner breath* holds the promise of human potential. On this journey, as self-knowledge expands, we come into a clearer recognition of the essential self.

Courage meets us at our outer edges and dares us to become who we truly are. From becoming to becoming, we create the unfolding story of our lives. Transformative growth rests upon what one makes of oneself. One cannot stay inside a closed system – of belief, of understanding, of vision.

Awareness, the source of our aliveness, is threefold: mindful self-presence, wise insight, sound judgment. Awareness sparks loving action and ignites being.

The inner breath of awareness serves as spiritual oxygen to draw forth one's true possibilities – it is the quality of attention one brings to the continuum of personal experience that is the basis for opening up a dimension of depth within self. A river of deep mind-body-spirit intelligence guides one's realization of meaning, and allows one's potential to breathe.

Time and again, life asks us to become who we are, to follow a path of passion and of purpose. Intention intersects with attention to enable us to claim personal power. By seeking out one's true direction of meaning, noble purpose is brought forth.

The hero is one who sets forth in search of moral integrity, enlarged consciousness, and the knowledge of what it means to live true to self. What the hero intends is to awaken wonder, passion, creativity, kindness, beauty, justice, and deep compassion.

Place yourself in the middle of the stream of
power and wisdom which flows into you as life,
place yourself in the full center of that flood,
then you are without effort impelled to truth,
to right, and a perfect contentment.

Ralph Waldo Emerson

There is a one-word antidote to thirst or craving:
wisdom – we can rediscover our innate wisdom,
awareness, and inner joy through spiritual
practices, including meditation, self-inquiry,
prayer, and the cultivation of our naturally
warm, tender, loving heart.
Wisdom is the means to transcend craving
and transform a treadmill existence into a lovely
inspiring garden walk. This is true freedom.

Lama Surya Das

What we have today is a demythologized
world – myths bring messages – they're
stories about the wisdom of life...
What we're learning in our schools is not
the wisdom of life. We're learning technologies,
we're getting information.

Joseph Campbell

It is true that neither the ancient wisdoms nor
the modern sciences are complete in themselves.
They do not stand alone. They call for one another.
Wisdom without science is unable to penetrate
the full sapiential meaning of the created
and material cosmos.
Science without wisdom leaves man enslaved
to a world of unrelated objects in which there
are no ways of discovering (or creating) order
and deep significance in man's pointless existence.
The vocation of modern man was to bring
about their union in preparation for a new age.

Thomas Merton

Again words express not merely
what we have found out for ourselves
but also all we care to learn from
the memories of other men, from
the common sense of the community,
from the pages of literature, from
the labors of scholars,
from the investigations of scientists,
from the experience of saints, from
the meditations of philosophers and
theologians.

   Bernard Lonergan

Sit in a room and read—and read and read.
And read the right books by the right people.
Your mind is brought onto that level, and
you have a nice, mild, slow-burning
rapture all the time.

   Joseph Campbell

If you receive my words, and treasure up
my commandments with you, making
your ear attentive to wisdom and
inclining your heart to understanding;
yes, if you cry out for insight, and raise
your voice for understanding, if you seek
it like silver, and search for it as for hidden
treasures; then you will understand the
fear of the Lord, and find the knowledge
of God.

—

Happy is the one who finds wisdom, and
the one who gets understanding, for
the gain from it is better than gain from
silver, and its profit better than gold.
She is more precious than jewels, and
nothing you desire can compare with her.
Long life is in her right hand; in her left
hand are riches and honour.
Her ways are ways of pleasantness, and
all her paths are peace. She is a tree of life
to those who lay hold of her; those
who hold her fast are called happy.

Proverbs 2:1-8, 3:13-18

Ordinary consciousness is not reflective
but rather a world of thoughts,
sensations, and feelings turning in
one direction, then another.
When it is utterly motionless, though,
consciousness becomes jewel-like,
reflective enough to help awareness
overcome this case of mistaken identity
and recognize its true nature. This, and
not our compulsive quest for gratification
from external experience, is the source of
the most profound happiness and wisdom.

Chip Hartranft

The discovery of truth is a pure joy to man
– it is liberation of his mind.
For a mere fact is like a blind lane;
it leads only to itself – it has no beyond.
But a truth opens up a whole horizon,
it leads us to the infinite.

Rabindranath Tagore

I can scarcely wait till tomorrow
when a new life begins for me,
as it does each day,
as it does each day.

Stanley Kunitz

And alone and without his nest
shall the eagle fly across the sun.

Kahlil Gibran

The feeling, this is not a part of me,
soon becomes, this is not what I want.
—
You soon realize that there's a difference
between the world you're living in and
the world you want to live in.

Northrop Frye

I am being driven forward
Into an unknown land.
The pass grows steeper,
The air colder and sharper.
A wind from my unknown goal
Stirs the strings of expectation.

The longest journey
Is the journey inwards.
Of him who has chosen his destiny,
Who has started upon his quest
For the source of his being.

Never look down to test the ground
before taking your next step:
only he who keeps his eye fixed on
the far horizon will find his right road.

What you have to attempt – to be
yourself. What you have to pray for
– to become a mirror in which,
according to the degree of purity you
have attained, the greatness of life
will be reflected.

Life only demands of you the strength
you possess. Only one feat is possible
– not to have run away.

Dag Hammarskjöld

The importance of process is another discovery.
Goals and endpoints matter less.
Learning is more urgent than storing information.
Caring is better than keeping.
Means are ends. The journey is the destination.
We begin to see the ways in which we have
postponed life, never paying attention to
the moment.
When life becomes a process, the old distinctions
between winning and losing, success and failure,
fade away. Everything, even a negative outcome,
has the potential to teach us and to further
our quest.
We are experimenting, exploring. In the wider
paradigm there are no 'enemies', only those useful,
if irritating, people whose opposition calls
attention to trouble spots, like a magnifying mirror.

Marilyn Ferguson

The goal ever recedes from us.
The greater the progress, the greater
the recognition of our unworthiness.
Satisfaction lies in the effort, not
in the attainment. Full effort is full victory.

Mahatma Gandhi

In every age, men have set off on pilgrimages,
on spiritual journeys, on personal quests.
Driven by pain, drawn by longing, lifted by hope,
singly and in groups they come in search
of relief, enlightenment, peace, power, joy
or they know not what.

Sheldon B. Kopp

There is the Islamic story of a pilgrim on the road
to Mecca. He is traveling on his long and difficult
journey bearing its many hardships, the privations
of hunger and thirst, extremes of weather, the
dangers of highwaymen. In the midst of his journey
he finds himself thinking of how very long and
difficult a journey it is.
The sufferings he is enduring make him keenly
aware that a great distance still remains to be
traveled before he will reach the holy place
of Mecca. Suddenly a light appears to him
and a voice speaks to him upon the road saying,
"Mecca is here, Mecca is now":
The road he is traveling is the goal he is seeking.
Mecca is the road, or more exactly, Mecca is the
quality of the desire with which he travels the road.

Ira Progoff

The newer the next stage, the more completely
it requires an abandonment of the old. We cannot
attain to it by any hasty movement of the surface
will. A growing tree can be broken by a sudden
gust. Its shape of growth can only be changed
by slow and constant pressure.
As the artist must wait with unstrained
attention until the tide of inspiration rises,
after which he must ride it to his goal,
so today, those who would forward
evolution can neither command nor neglect
the inner drive. Coerced, it recoils; unattended,
it dies down.
The whole of life must, therefore, be directed to
this end. Wide room must be found for watching
and learning the flow of this current and how,
when it sets, to take it at the flood and make
the voyage to new levels.

Gerald Heard

One word itself here before any other:
you must 'simplify' your life.
You have a difficult journey before you...
do not burden yourself with too much luggage.

A.D. Sertillanges

...your entire life journey ultimately consists
of the steps you are taking at this moment.
There is always only this one step, and so
you give it your fullest attention.
This doesn't mean you don't know where
you are going; it just means this step
is primary, the destination secondary.
And what you encounter at your destination
once you get there depends on the quality
of this one step. Another way of putting it:
what the future holds for you depends
on your state of consciousness now.

Eckhart Tolle

Life itself will purify our hopes step by step if
we live with a passion for the possible. As we
go forward, the apparent limits of the possible
will be pushed back further and further into
the region of the seemingly impossible.
Sooner or later we realize the possible has no
fixed limits. What we mistook for a limit proves
to be a horizon. And, like every horizon, it
recedes as we move on toward fullness of life.

David Steindl-Rast

Don't ask what the world needs.
Ask what makes you come alive,
and go do it.
Because what the world needs
is people who have come alive.

Howard Thurman

Precisely because you are aware of the limits
of life, you are compelled to bring forth what
is within you; this is the only time you have
to show yourself.
You can't hold back or hide in a cave, you can't
waste away in a meaningless job, cramming
your life with trivia; the drama of the cosmic
story won't allow it.
The supreme insistence of life is that you enter
the adventure of creating yourself. Each instant
of your life has been folded into unnameable
significance; all rests on your self-creativity,
for out of you comes forth ultimate reality.
The dynamics that fashioned the stars are now
brought into your self-reflective awareness,
and what they create is your free adventure,
your surprise for the universe.

Brian Swimme

Awakening from this dream, he was overwhelmed
by a great feeling of sadness. It seemed to him that
he had spent his life in a worthless and senseless
manner; he retained nothing vital, nothing
in any way precious or worthwhile. He stood alone,
like a shipwrecked man on the shore.
Sadly, Siddhartha went to a pleasure garden that
belonged to him, closed the gates, sat under a
mango tree, and felt horror and death in his heart.
Gradually, he collected his thoughts and mentally
went through the whole of his life, from the earliest
days which he could remember. When had he really
been happy? When had he really experienced joy?
Then he felt in his heart: a path lies before you
which you are called to follow. The gods await you.

Hermann Hesse

We didn't see the seven mountains ahead of us.
We didn't see how they are always ahead, always
calling us, always reminding us that there are more
things to be done, dreams to be realized, joys to be
rediscovered, promises made before birth to be
fulfilled, beauty to be incarnated, and love
embodied. We didn't notice how they hinted that
nothing is ever finished, that struggles are never
truly concluded, that sometimes we have
to re-dream our lives, and that life can always be
used to create more light...

Ben Okri

But whether small or great, and no matter
what the stage and grade of life, the call
rings up the curtain, always, on a mystery
of transfiguration – a rite, or moment, of
spiritual passage, which when complete,
amounts to a dying and a birth.
The familiar life horizon has been outgrown;
the old concepts, ideals, and emotional
patterns no longer fit; the time for the
passing of a threshold is at hand.

Joseph Campbell

I don't know who – or what – put the question,
I don't know when it was put. I don't even
remember answering. But at some moment
I did answer *Yes* to Someone – or Something –
and from that hour I was certain that existence
is meaningful and that, therefore, my life,
in self-surrender, had a goal.

Dag Hammarskjöld

Each man has his own vocation.
The talent is the call.
There is one direction in which all space
is open to him. He has faculties silently
inviting him thither to endless exertion.
He is like a ship in a river; he runs against
obstructions on every side but one; on
that side all obstruction is taken away,
and he sweeps serenely over
a deepening channel into an infinite sea.

Ralph Waldo Emerson

Of the many callings in the world, the
invitation to the adventure of an awakened
and full life is the most exhilarating.
This is the dream of every heart. Yet most
of us are lost or caught in forms of life
that exile us from the life we dream of.
Most people long to step onto the path
of creative change that would awaken
their lives to beauty and passion, deepen
their contentment, and allow their lives
to make a difference.

John O'Donohue

...there is a will within each of us,
quite outside the range of conscious control,
a will which knows what is right for us,
which is repeatedly reporting to us
via our bodies, emotions, and dreams,
and is incessantly encouraging
our healing and wholeness.
We are all called to keep this appointment
with the inner life, and many of us never do.
Fortunately, this insistent invitation comes
to us again and again.

James Hollis

How do we best respond to the inner
restlessness that resides in the tension
between what is and what is yet to be?
For each of us, an epic journey of learning
and loving unfolds out of life's endless summons
to transformation – the invitation to live
more consciously, more creatively,
more compassionately.
Obedience to that summons brings us into
the blissful experience of human authenticity.

Stephen Sims

What happens in an individual when we
first feel that something deeper within
ourselves is calling to us, trying to see us,
not only from the past but from the future
– a future we cannot even imagine
in the midst of our crowded, complicated
minutes, hours and days, but which is
in fact what we are really starving for
when we are starved for time?

Jacob Needleman

Still, our actions and devoted enthusiasms
seem to set up something akin to a magnetic
field that draws to us benedictions and
resources that can help us realize the calling.
…opportunities wash up on shore; people
take an interest; out of the corner of your eye,
you spy synchronicities; the right book or
the right person crosses your path. Sometimes
even the money follows. Perhaps it's nothing
more mysterious than the universe supporting
growth, and life loving itself.

Gregg Levoy

When the Guest is being searched for,
it is the intensity of the longing
for the Guest that does all the work.
Look at me, and
you will see a slave of that intensity.

Kabir

That which you are seeking
is also seeking you.

Jalal al-Din Rumi

…wholeness of personality is not a goal
that is off in the future; it is a condition
of being that becomes present
in the course of the work that seeks it.

Ira Progoff

Three deep cravings of the self...
The first is the craving which makes him
a pilgrim and wanderer. It is the longing
to go out from his normal world in search
of a lost home, a *better country*...
The next is that craving of heart for heart,
of the soul for its perfect mate, which makes
him a lover.
The third is the craving for inward purity
and perfection, which makes him an ascetic,
and in the last resort a saint.

Evelyn Underhill

Not only are our bodies erotic, our spirits
are erotic too. Or rather we are body-spirits
and the energies of desire permeate our being.
The desires and longings which we have
for what is beautiful, for what makes sense,
for what is true, for what has value, and
for what has ultimate value are at the heart
of what it means to be human.

Vernon Gregson

Human striving reflects a whole gamut of desire,
– from basic physical needs to the deeper
longings of the heart.

Certain drives focus on survival, sexual fulfillment,
and the acquisition of power. On the spiritual level,
we experience a thirst for self-knowledge and
wisdom, and a strong yearning for love.
In search of the essential self, our desires often
pull us in different directions, and compete with
one another. It then becomes necessary to sort
out these different drives, and evaluate
our choices in terms of their congruence with
values that lead us to true freedom.

—

We have then to awaken a fascination for
self-discovery that energizes transformation,
for it is the longing for wholeness that drives us
to plumb our inner depth.
In observing the flow of other happenings and
inner experience, and probing the yet unknown,
our lives become defined by an aspiration
for enlarged consciousness.

Stephen K. Sims

We do not yet possess ourselves,
and we know at the same time
that we are much more.

Ralph Waldo Emerson

Within us we have a hope that always walks
in front of our present narrow experience...
Consciously or unconsciously, we have in our
life this feeling of Truth which is ever larger than
its appearance, for our life is facing the infinite,
and it is in movement.
Its aspiration is therefore infinitely more than
its achievement, and as it goes on it finds that
no realization of truth ever leaves it stranded
on the desert of finality, but carries it to
a region beyond.

Rabindranath Tagore

I am but a poor struggling soul and yearning
to be wholly good – wholly truthful and wholly
non-violent in thought, word and deed; but ever
failing to reach the ideal which I know to be true.
It is a painful climb, but the pain of it is a positive
pleasure to me. Each step upward makes me
feel stronger and fit for the next.

Mahatma Gandhi

You are good in countless ways, and you are not
evil when you are not good,
You are only loitering and sluggard.
Pity that the stags cannot teach swiftness to
the turtles. In your longing for your giant self lies
your goodness: and that longing is in all of you.
But in some of you that longing is a torrent
rushing with might to the sea, carrying the secrets
of the hillsides and the songs of the forest. And
in others it is a flat stream that loses itself in angles
and bends and lingers before it reaches the shore.
But let not him who longs much say to him who
longs little, 'Wherefore are you slow and halting?'
For the truly good ask not the naked,
'Where is your garment?' nor the homeless,
'What has befallen your house?'

Kahlil Gibran

You do not know what you can do,
or who you are in your fullest significance,
or what powers are hiding within you.
All exists in the emptiness of your potentiality,
a realm that cannot be seen or tasted or touched.
How will you bring these powers forth?
How will you awaken your creativity?
By responding to the allurements that beckon
to you, by following your passions and interests.
Alluring activity draws you into being,
just as it drew the stars into being.
Our life and powers come forth
through our response to allurement.

Brian Swimme

...if you do follow your bliss you put yourself
on a kind of track that has been there
all the while, waiting for you, and the life that
you ought to be living is the one you are living.
When you can see that, you begin to meet
people who are in the field of your bliss,
and they open the doors to you.
I say, follow your bliss and don't be afraid,
and doors will open where you didn't know
they were going to be.

Joseph Campbell

Friend, wake up! Why do you go on sleeping?
The night is over – do you want to lose
the day the same way?
Others who managed to get up early
have already found an elephant or a jewel.
My inside, listen to me, the greatest spirit,
the Teacher is near, wake up, wake up!
You have slept for millions and millions of years.
Why not wake up this morning?

Kabir

Is there anything I can do
to make myself enlightened?
As little as you can do to make
the sun rise in the morning.
Then of what use are the spiritual
exercises you prescribe?
To make sure you are not asleep
when the sun begins to rise.

Zen Master – disciple

Somewhere out at the edges, the night
Is turning and the waves of darkness
Begin to brighten the shore of dawn.
The heavy dark falls back to earth
And the freed air goes wild with light,
The heart fills with fresh, bright breath
And thoughts stir to give birth to colour.

I arise today

In the name of Silence,
Womb of the Word,
In the name of Stillness,
Home of Belonging,
In the name of the Solitude
of the Soul and the Earth.

I arise today

Blessed by all things,
Wings of breath,
Delight of eyes,
Wonder of whisper,
Intimacy of touch,
Eternity of soul,
Urgency of thought,
Miracle of health,
Embrace of God.
May I live this day
Compassionate of heart,
Gentle in word,
Gracious in awareness,
Courageous in thought,
Generous in love.

John O'Donohue

And this is the simple truth – that to live
is to feel oneself lost –
he who accepts it has already begun
to find himself, to be on firm ground.
(H)e who does not really feel himself lost,
is without remission;
that is to say, he never finds himself,
never comes up against his own reality.

José Ortega y Gasset

An experience of awakening is a moment
of self-recognition when one is graced with
deeper insight into the path and purpose
of one's life.
Such revelations imply a transformed vision
of where one's life wants to go. They fortify
individual integrity by placing focus on
essential meaning.
Human frustration pushes towards freedom
and fulfillment. There arises a determination
that becomes indispensable to the journey
towards the integrity for which we hunger.

Stephen K. Sims

Disasters and failures, tragedy and catastrophe,
never have the final word;
in fact, they often foster the preconditions
that lead to a new evolutionary outburst.

Diarmuid O'Murchu

Given the proper circumstances, the human
brain has boundless capacities for paradigm
shifts. It can order and reorder itself,
integrate, transcend old conflicts.
Anything that disrupts the old order of our lives
has the potential for triggering a transformation,
a movement toward greater maturity,
openness, strength. Sometimes the perturbing
element is obvious stress: a job loss, a divorce,
serious illness, financial troubles, a death in the
family, imprisonment, even sudden success or
a promotion. Or it may be subtle intellectual stress:
a close relationship with someone whose views
differ markedly from those we have always held;
a book that shakes our belief; or a new
environment, a foreign country.

Marilyn Ferguson

Awakening brings its own assignments,
unique to each of us
–you are a seed, a silent promise.

Marilyn Ferguson

The emancipation of our physical nature
is in attaining health, of our social being in
attaining goodness, and of our self in attaining
love. This last is what Buddha describes as
extinction–the extinction of selfishness –
which is the function of love, and which does
not lead to darkness but to illumination.
This is the attainment of bodhi, or the true
awakening; it is the revealing in us of
the infinite joy by the light of love.

Rabindranath Tagore

Once you awaken to a certain point,
you don't ask for suffering;
but when suffering comes, you work with it.
You see the way in which suffering
is the grace that forces your awakening.

Ram Dass

Times are difficult globally; awakening is no
longer a luxury or an ideal. It's becoming critical.
We don't need to add more depression, more
discouragement, or more anger to what's already
here. It's becoming essential that we learn how
to relate sanely with difficult times.
The earth seems to be beseeching us to connect
with joy and discover our innermost essence.
This is the best way that we can benefit others.
We can use everything that happens to us as
a means for waking up.
We can use everything that occurs – whether
it's our conflicting emotions and thoughts or
our seemingly outer situation – to show us
where we are asleep and how we can wake up
completely, utterly, without reservations.

Pema Chodron

The breeze at dawn
Has secrets to tell you.
Don't go back to sleep.

Jalal al-Din Rumi

I would like to live
Like a river flows
Carried by the surprise
Of its own unfolding.

John O'Donohue

Practicing the edge means constantly
paying attention to our hopes, fears
and dreams, and pushing ourselves
to whatever is next.
Practicing the edge requires constantly
leaving behind the known, secure and
familiar for the unknown that seems,
somehow, to beckon.

Robert Jingen Gunn

At a dinner party many years ago, I sat next
to a man who was an oceanographer.
At one point he asked me if I had ever wondered
why lobsters could weigh one pound, three
pounds, even ten pounds when they had such
a hard shell – how could they grow?
I had to tell him this was a problem that was
not very high on my list of priorities. He smiled
and proceeded to tell me that when a lobster
becomes crowded in its shell and can't grow
anymore, by instinct it travels out to some place
in the sea, hoping for relative safety, and begins
to shed its shell. It is a terribly dangerous
process – the lobster has to risk its life, because
once it becomes naked, vulnerable, it can be
dashed against a reef or eaten by another lobster
or fish. But that is the only way it can grow.

Eda LeShan

The snake that cannot shed its skin must perish.

Friedrich Nietzsche

A complex structure is connected at many points
and in many ways. ... Because these connections
can only be sustained by a flow of energy,
the system is always in flux. Notice the paradox;
the more coherent or intricately connected
the structure, the more unstable it is.
Increased coherence means increased instability!
This very instability is the key to transformation.
The continuous movement of energy through
the system results in fluctuations; if they are minor,
the system damps them and they do not alter
its structural integrity. But if the fluctuations reach
a critical size, they *perturb* the system.
They increase the number of novel interactions
within it. They shake it up. The elements of
the old pattern come in contact with each other
in new ways and make new connections.
The parts reorganize into a new whole.
The system escapes into a higher order.
The more complex or coherent a structure,
the greater the next level of complexity.
Each transformation makes the next one likelier.
Each new level is even more integrated and
connected than the one before, requiring a
greater flow of energy for maintenance, and
is therefore still less stable. To put it another
way, flexibility begets flexibility.

Marilyn Ferguson

For the mythological hero is the champion
not of things become but of things becoming,
the dragon to be slain by him is precisely
the monster of the status quo:
Holdfast, the keeper of the past.

Joseph Campbell

Life must be continually given up
for greater life.

Joseph Chilton Pearce

Especially we fear becoming someone
we do not as yet know.
To liberate the desire for this becoming
is to come into the perfect love
that casts out fear.

Sebastian Moore

I associate the garden with the whole
experience of being alive, and so,
there is nothing in the range of human
experience that is separate from what
the garden can signify in its eagerness
and its insistence, and in its driving
energy to live – to grow, to bear fruit.

Stanley Kunitz

Even near the end of life everything
can come alive
in new and unforeseen forms.
The urgency, restlessness and passion
of youth are all there as though
everything is about to begin anew.

John O'Donohue

If there is no change in our consciousness
today, there will be no change in our outer
experience tomorrow.
In proportion, as some change takes place
in our consciousness, in that proportion there
is an improvement in our outer affairs – either
in health, personal relationships, or supply.
That which goes into consciousness must
come forth as manifestation.
Truth itself appears as manifestation.
Spirit is the substance, and the form
is its manifestation.

Joel Goldsmith

A new being springs forth from every fresh
contact. My nature opens and opens to
thousands of new influences. I feel countless
new births. Such is the glory of our
common everyday life.

Mary Parker Follet

Poetry as meta medium –
metabolic, metaphoric, metamorphic
– articulating shifts of being,
changes and transfers of energy.
Stanley Kunitz

When you change the way you look at things,
the things you look at change.
Max Planck

If we tried to come up with a central Jewish
metaphor to capture the way of the world,
it might be Chinese boxes.
There is an ebb and flow, but this flux,
like a box within a box,
resides within stability, and that stability
in turn resides within flux,
which resides within stability, and so on.

Avram Davis

You can change the next moment,
you can do something different;
something enlightened;
something creative, imaginative, and fresh;
something compassionate and wise.

Lama Surya Das

You can't stop the waves,
but you can learn to surf.

Jon Kabat-Zinn

We approach the future with a plan for it
precisely in the hope of escaping
the radical throes of it;
we hope to have a future that will not be
disruptive, disturbing, or deconstructive.

Jerome A. Miller

The summons of life is ever to go on growing,
to let go of attachments and leap over fear into
new possibility. Change inevitably presents itself
as an ordeal that engenders a degree of confusion
and chaos. Even so, the status quo must be
challenged over and over, allowing the human
spirit to move ever forward. Each leap of faith
involves a dying and a birth. The cost of any
defense against development is boredom and
banality, and an emptiness of meaning; any
prolonged resistance to change creates an impasse
in the psyche, a tension that sooner or later has to
give. What must be refused is the temptation to
become closed, to shut down possibility, to choose
complacency. Change is about facing difficult trials
and tests. It is about honesty, and cultivating
rigorous self-knowledge. It is about making hard
choices and letting go of secure routines.
Change requires a determination to be conscious.
Each threshold of change demands a letting go –
we are required to put certain elements of our
lives behind us in order to move forward.

Stephen K. Sims

Water is purified by flowing,
the human being by going forward.
Hindu proverb

No man ever steps in the same river twice,
for it's not the same river and
he's not the same man.
Heraclitus

What is clear – is that we certainly cannot
stay where we are and as we are.
Our individual selves, our culture, our society
and our race – all are profoundly unstable
and rapidly becoming more unstable.
However we try to escape it, we come back
to the same point: we must go on or collapse.
Gerald Heard

The word 'ecstasy' comes from 'e' (out) and
'stasis' (a state of standstill). To be ecstatic
literally means to be out of a static place.
Thus those who live ecstatic lives are always
moving away from rigidly fixed situations and
exploring new and unexplored aspects of reality.
Here we see the essence of joy. Joy is always
new. Whereas there can be old pain, old grief,
and old sorrow, there can be no old joy.
Old joy is not joy. Joy is always connected with
movement, renewal, rebirth, change – in short,
with life. Joy is essentially ecstatic since it moves
out of the place of death, which is rigid and fixed,
into the place of life, which is new and surprising.

Henri J.M. Nouwen

In nature every moment is new, the past is always
swallowed and forgotten; becoming only is sacred.
Nothing is secure but life, transition, the energizing
spirit. No love can be bound by oath or covenant to
secure it against a higher love. No truth so sublime
but it may be trivial tomorrow in the light of new
thoughts. People wish to be settled; only as far as
they are unsettled is there any hope for them.

Ralph Waldo Emerson

When the whole grows, it multiplies its
interrelationships, upsetting the status quo,
absorbing new cells; and the elements break
up the previous cohesion.
And this goes on continually: every 'position'
is continually shifting. Like a close-knit group,
when a new member is introduced, the
group must die to its previous harmony and
include a disrupting agent – a move which
precisely, if it is well integrated, will produce
a greater comprehension, a broader view,
a more encompassing consciousness, a
more universal growth.
Thus, concludes Prigogine, a minimum
of instability alone guarantees growth; and
the more there is instability (without upsetting
the total balance or metabolism), the more
there is a chance for growth.
This law is applicable to the spiritual path:
one can only grow by outgrowing.
One stagnates and suffers by clinging.
One must continually let go.

Placide Gaboury

God grant me the serenity to accept the things
I cannot change, the courage to change the things
I can, and the wisdom to know the difference.

The Serenity Prayer

Unclose your mind.
You are not a prisoner.
You are a bird in flight,
searching the skies for dreams.
Haruki Murakami

You have everything you need
to build something far bigger than yourself.
Seth Godin

First say to yourself
what you would be;
and then do
what you have to do.
Epictetus

Molecules and stars, brainwaves and concepts,
individuals and societies – all have the potential
for transformation.
Transformation, like a vehicle on a downward
incline, gathers momentum as it goes. All
wholes transcend their parts by virtue of internal
coherence, cooperation, openness to input.
The higher on the evolutionary scale, the more
freedom to reorganize. An ant lives out a destiny;
a human being shapes one.
Evolution is a continuous breaking and forming
to make new, richer wholes. Even our genetic
material is in flux.
If we try to live as closed systems, we are doomed
to regress. If we enlarge our awareness, admit
new information, and take advantage of the
brain's brilliant capacity to integrate and reconcile,
we can leap forward.

Marilyn Ferguson

It often happens that the potentialities
in the individual do not wait silently
for their opportunity to emerge; but that
they press, strain, clamor, disturb the entire
personality until an avenue of expression
is opened for them.

Ira Progoff

One can enter the process to reach into
the depth of the psyche to where the seed
of potentiality is pressing toward growth.
One can touch that seed there to evoke
its strength and to generate a momentum
that will enable the person to move forward
to the next stage of development, and
eventually to the further stage of conflict that
must inevitably follow in the cycles of growth.
The important point in carrying this through
successfully is to refrain deliberately from
premature diagnosis.
When symptoms of disturbance appear where
these symptoms are part of the process of
personal growth, the meaning and potentiality
of development is missed if it is interpreted in
the light of pathology.
One reason is that when a person begins
to think of himself in the light of pathology
his image grows dim. The thoughts he protects
are thoughts of weakness and they refer to
the difficulties experienced along the road
of development rather than to the unfolding
essence of the process as a whole.

Ira Progoff

A seed holds a silent promise – the possibility
of what it can become when fully matured.
Its power to grow is generated from within, but,
of course, it must be planted in an environment
that enables its growth.
Seeds have an eagerness to grow, and bear
fruit. Each contains a direction of development,
and draws forth its maturation through
a sequence of transformations. Over time,
as a seed releases its latent potential, it reveals
fields of possibility not previously evident.
Similar to a seed, the gift that one's life
represents awaits maturation and manifestation.
The principle of growth expresses itself in
a thrust towards the realization of the true self.
We are moved toward something greater, and
in order to discover our higher possibilities,
it is necessary to push beyond routine expectations
of self. As we come into contact with the
essence of who we are, are we able to refine
our understanding of what it means to live
a genuine life.

Stephen K. Sims

Throughout history, man's supposed limitations
have given way before the power of the human
imagination, the ability of the human intellect
to conceive of and do what has never been done
before. The vision of life as it ought to be acts
as a powerful magnet in the advance of
the human race.
Pessimism operates in a narrowed field of vision
that fails to take into account the possibilities
at the outer edges of experience.

Norman Cousins

We must be willing to get rid of the life
we've planned, so as to have the life that
is waiting for us.

Joseph Campbell

They may be able to resist seeing the vision,
and even when they see it, the cost of entering
into it through an altered life may seem prohibitive.
We know that discovery can be made, and must
be demonstrated and that those who perceive it
and adhere to it, find, not only the cost insignificant,
but the life so disclosed to be a reality besides
which the life left behind was a stifling shadow.

Gerald Heard

Before I can tell my life
what I want to do with it,
I must listen to my life
telling me who I am.

Parker Palmer

Yes, wonderfully, exhilaratingly, we have
this extraordinary capacity for good.
Fundamentally, we are good; we are made
for love, for compassion, for caring, for sharing,
for peace and reconciliation, for transcendence,
for the beautiful, for the true and the good.

Desmond Tutu

Every man's foremost task is the actualization
of his unique, unprecedented
and never-recurring potentialities.

Martin Buber

You must learn to get in touch with
the innermost essence of your being.
This true essence is beyond the ego.
It is fearless; it is free;
it is immune to criticism;
it does not fear any challenge.
It is beneath no one, superior to no one,
and full of magic, mystery, and
enchantment.

Deepak Chopra

The essential self is bigger than the ego
self. The ego displays grasping and greed,
and lasts but for a time.
In contrast, the essential self dwells
in goodness and generosity for all time.

Stephen Sims

If you look too closely at form,
You miss the essence.

Jalal al-Din Rumi

Small Mind, or deluded mind, is the buzzing,
unpredictable, frequently out-of-control
ordinary mind. This is our finite mind, or
limited conceptual mind; our ordinary,
rational, discursive, thinking mind.
The deluded mind has so many impulses and
needs; it wants so many things. It's frequently
confused; it's subject to mood swings;
it's restless. It gets angry; it gets depressed;
it becomes hyper.
What is meant by Big Mind is the essential
nature of mind itself. This is what we call
Buddha-nature, or natural mind. This is our
true nature – the pure boundless awareness
that is at the heart, and part, of us all.
The Buddha described it as still, clear, lucid,
empty, profound, simple (uncomplicated)
and at peace. It's not really what we usually
think of as our mind at all. It is the
luminous, most fundamental clear
light nature of our ground of being.

Lama Surya Das

The collective disease of humanity is that people
are so engrossed in what happens, so hypnotized
by the world of fluctuating forms, so absorbed
in the content of their lives, they have forgotten
the essence, that which is beyond content,
beyond form, beyond thought.
They are so consumed by time that they have
forgotten eternity, which is their origin, their
home, their destiny. Eternity is the living reality
of who you are.
Once there is a certain degree of Presence, of still
and alert attention in human beings' perceptions,
they can sense the divine life essence, the one
indwelling consciousness or spirit in every creature,
every life-form, recognize it as one with their own
essence and so love it as themselves.
Until this happens, however, most humans
see only the outer forms, unaware of the inner
essence, just as they are unaware
of their own essence and identify only with
their own physical and psychological form.

Eckhart Tolle

At the center there is a stillness – there,
your essential self exists:
the permanent being which persists through
and beyond the flow and change
of your conscious states.
Retreat to that point whence all various
lines of your activities flow, and to which
at last they may return.
This is a practical recipe, not a pious
exhortation. The thing may sound absurd to you,
but you can do it if you will: standing back as it
were, from the vague and purposeless reactions
in which most men fritter their vital energies.
Then you can survey with a certain calm, a certain
detachment, your universe and the possibilities
of life within it.
This universe, these possibilities, are far richer,
yet far simpler than you have supposed.
Seen from the true centre of personality, instead
of the usual angle of self-interest,
their scattered parts arrange themselves in order:
you begin to perceive those graduated levels
of Reality with which a purified and intensified
consciousness can unite.

Evelyn Underhill

I know only that I was born and exist, and
it seems to me that I have been carried
along. I exist on the foundation of something
I do not know. In spite of all uncertainties,
I feel a solidity underlying all existence and
a continuity in my mode of being.

Carl Jung

The most profound tendency of the psyche
is to represent itself…this self-representation
means that we are almost overburdened with
clues about our own nature. By natural, I mean
those consistent realities of our experience
that transcend our manipulations.
These natural tendencies or directions within
point beyond our limited understanding
to realities we are embedded in.
Indeed, our natural tendencies make us.
…A single dramatic theme can stand in the
background of one's life for a whole lifetime,
awaiting expression.

Wilson Van Dusen

I am obviously free.
But what does my freedom represent other than
an imperceptible point buried in an indeterminate
mass of laws and relationships that I cannot,
by and large, control?
All I can do is shrewdly make what use I may
of them, follow their slant, sail with their wind,
appear to master them and bend them to my will
— when all I am, in fact, doing is to set them off
one against the other.
Each one of us can distinguish in the depths of his
being a whole system of deep-seated tendencies
— a law of his own individual evolution — that
nothing can suppress and that persists through
every stage of greater perfection.
This personal driving force is prior to and higher
than free will; it is written into our character,
into the rhythm of our thoughts, and into the
crude surge of our passions; and it is life's
heritage to us, it is the conscious evidence in us
of the vast vital current, one trickle of which
forms us; it is our subjection to the great task
of development of which we, for one brief hour,
are no more than the artisans.

Teilhard de Chardin

…when a man is so utterly stripped
of life meaning…he has no furnishings
for his inner life; he is as good as dead,
even though his organism gropes blindly
toward life…organisms live by bread,
but man lives by meaning.

Ernest Becker

As far as we can discern, the sole
purpose of human existence is to kindle
a light of meaning in the darkness
of mere being.
Your vision will become clear only
when you look into your heart –
Who looks outside, dreams.
Who looks inside, awakens.

Carl Jung

Pain is always real – though its cause may
not be physiological. If left so, the patient's
pain will continue to work until it causes
physiological change. Its cause, while still
psychological, must be diagnosed.
The patient is told to watch his way of living,
asked whether he is worrying, whether he is
anxious and thwarted. Such advice may not,
indeed seldom can, arrest pain and make it
cease to gnaw till it destroys tissues.
The patient, as one of these diagnosticians
remarked, generally needs no operation,
no medicinal treatment.
But he does need something very badly and,
if he fails to get it in time, he will be back in
the surgeon's hands, this time with something
that a surgeon can see. He needs a different
life, a life of purpose and of meaning to raise
him out of his growing and gnawing sense
of futility, frustration and inevitable failure.
—

There is meaning, and that meaning can
be found. The way to that meaning is through
tender loving kindness, for the open mind
depends upon the open heart.

Gerald Heard

A major part of the meaning of life is contained
in the very process of discovering it.
It is an ongoing experience of growth
that involves a deepening of contact with reality.
The tendency is observed throughout the
natural world that individual beings are drawn
in the direction that fulfills the potentialities
of their nature. The psyche is the faculty by
means of which this occurs. When the principle
of meaning, which the psyche embodies,
is experienced intensely by an individual,
it has the effect of opening in him a sensitivity
to meaningfulness not only in his personal life
but in the universe around him.

Ira Progoff

To respond to the call of authenticity is to put
oneself in a position of openness – one must
step into the unknown. Increasingly drawn by
the power of wonder, new leaps of learning
connect us to our hidden selves.
Questions arise that guide us into a new vision
of reality, and challenge us to remain open to
the unexpected – to the surprise of who we are.
The big question life asks each of us is:
what am I here to do?

Stephen K. Sims

I have frequently seen people become neurotic
when they content themselves with inadequate
or wrong answers to the questions of life. They
seek position, marriage, reputation, outward
success or money, and remain unhappy and
neurotic even when they have attained what
they were seeking. Such people are usually
contained within too narrow a spiritual horizon.
Their life has not sufficient content, sufficient
meaning. If they are enabled to develop into
more spacious personalities, the neurosis
generally disappears.
The meaning of my existence is that life has
addressed a question to me. Or, conversely,
I myself am a question which is addressed to
the world, and I must communicate my answer,
for otherwise I am dependent upon the
world's answer.
That is a supra personal life task, which
I accomplish only by effort and with difficulty.

Carl Jung

The bankruptcy of modern psychology is its flight
from the soul, and therefore from the transcendent
task of meaning. Such a denial of depth is a failure
of nerve in the face of largeness.

James Hollis

There is nothing in the world, I venture to say,
that would so effectively help one to survive even
the worst conditions as the knowledge that there
is a meaning in one's life.
As each situation in life represents a challenge
to man and presents a problem for him
to solve, the question of the meaning
of life may actually be reversed.
Ultimately, man should not ask what the
meaning of his life is, but rather he must
recognize that it is *he* who is asked.
In a word, each man is questioned by life;
and he can only answer to life by answering
for his own life; to life he can only respond
by being responsible.
Thus, logotherapy seesin responsibleness
the very essence of human existence.

—

According to logotherapy, we can discover
meaning in life in three different ways:
(i) by creating a work or doing a deed;
(ii) by experiencing something or encountering
someone; and (iii) by the attitude we take
toward unavoidable suffering.

The first, the way of achievement or
accomplishment is quite obvious. The second
way of finding meaning in life is by experiencing
something – such as goodness, truth and beauty –
by experiencing nature and culture or, last but
not least, by experiencing another human being
in his very uniqueness – by loving him...
We must never forget that we may also find
meaning in life even when confronted with
a hopeless situation, when facing a fate
that cannot be changed.
For what then matters is to bear witness to
the uniquely human potential at its best, which
is to transform a personal tragedy into a triumph,
to turn one's predicament into a human
achievement. When we are no longer able
to change the situation – just think of an
incurable disease such as an inoperable cancer
– we are challenged to change ourselves.

Viktor E. Frankl

Every blade of grass has an angel
that bends over it and whispers:
grow, grow.

The Talmud

Enhanced awareness promotes in all of us
the traits that abound in the creative person:
whole-seeing, fresh childlike perceptions,
playfulness, a sense of flow, risk-taking;
the ability to focus attention in a relaxed way,
to become lost in the object of contemplation;
the ability to deal with many complex ideas
at the same time, willingness to diverge from
the prevailing view; access to preconscious
material; seeing what is there rather than
what is expected or conditioned.
The transformed self has new tools, gifts,
sensibilities. Like an artist, it spies patterns;
it finds meaning and its own, inescapable
originality. (L)ike a good scientist, the
transformed self experiments, speculates,
invents, and relishes the unexpected.

Marilyn Ferguson

Creative Being...
is being unfinished, is being you, is becoming you;
is developing your abilities to anticipate, recognize,
understand, manage, create and enjoy changes;
is being curious, seeking to find out, just to know;
is learning to unlearn;
is being aware;
is being aware of not being aware;
is being aware of what has been and
being appreciative of what could be;
is being aware that there is more to see,
more to know, more to understand, more to do;
is bringing things into being: music, paintings,
loving relationships, beautiful friendships,
crazy dreams, impossible ideas;
is always learning; is being, loving.

Milton Dawes

The human mind-brain system is designed for
functions radically different from and broader than
its current uses. An astonishing capacity for creative
power is built into our genes, ready to unfold.
Our innate capacities of mind are nothing less
than miraculous, and we are born with a driving
intent to express this capacity.

Joseph Chilton Pearce

In one way or another, life is always urging us
to dare our dreams.
Beyond injury and entrapment and victimization,
beyond all the constrictions of past and present,
there is a freedom that is won when we avoid
locking personal identity into a notion that is
defined by powerlessness.

Stephen K. Sims

Growth is a death on my youth laid…
I had determined to move on – to linger
would be to lose.

Dan Berrigan

The concrete being of man, then, is being in process.
His existing lies in developing.
His unrestricted desire to know heads him
ever towards a known unknown.

Bernard Lonergan

The spiritual path is an adventure in growth.
There is a law of growth which is universal.
Growth is painful; growth is incompatible
with a search for security and stability, or
a defence of what is acquired and established.

Placide Gaboury

I knew that I wanted
to learn more,
not earn more.

Lama Surya Das

The first year that I engaged in intentional
personal growth, I discovered that it was going
to be a lifetime process.
During that year, the question in my mind
changed from 'How long will this take?'
to 'How far can I go?'

John C. Maxwell

Development is a matter of increasing the number
of things that one does for oneself, that one
decides for oneself, that one finds out for oneself.
There is a critical point in the increasing autonomy
of the subject. It is reached when the subject finds
out for himself that it is up to him to decide what
he is to make of himself.
…This making oneself is open-eyed, deliberate.
Autonomy decides what autonomy is to be.
The opposite to this open-eyed, deliberate self-
control is drifting. The drifter has not yet found
himself; he has not yet discovered his own deed
and so is content to do what everybody else
is doing; he has not yet discovered his own will
and so he is content to choose what everyone else
is choosing; he has not yet discovered a mind of
his own and so he is content to think and say
what everyone else is thinking and saying;
and the others too are apt to be drifters, each
of them doing and choosing and thinking
and saying what others happen to be doing,
choosing, thinking, saying.

Bernard Lonergan

It is only by rowing oneself that one goes
forward; no current can take you to the point
you aim at reaching.
Go your own way and do not drift into
the wake of everybody else.

A.D. Sertillanges

Live poetically! – that is, make a work of art
out of the elements of your life.
If the universe is in a state of development,
what is the goal of this process? And what
is the structure of the developmental change?
The goal of the process is for the universe to
become a subject; that is, to become autonomous
and self-knowing; that is, to become free.
Think of a human fetus. It is almost purely
vegetative, but through a process of development
it becomes sentient, then conscious, then
knowing, and then self-knowing, and lastly
aware of the fact that it is self-aware.

John Douglas Mullen

The material body is a river of atoms,
the mind is a river of thought,
and what holds them together is a river
of intelligence.

Deepak Chopra

Do you have a body?
Don't sit on the porch!
Go out and walk in the rain.

Kabir

There's one thing that,
when cultivated and regularly practiced,
leads to deep spiritual intention,
to peace,
to mindfulness and clear comprehension,
to vision and knowledge,
to a happy life here and now, and
to the culmination of wisdom and awakening.
And what is that one thing?
It is mindfulness centered on the body.

Buddha

The body's intelligence is – an inseparable part
of universal intelligence, one of its countless
manifestations. It gives temporary cohesion to the
atoms and molecules that make up your physical
organism.
It is the organizing principle behind the workings
of all the organs of the body, the conversion
of oxygen and food into energy, the heartbeat and
circulation of the blood, the immune system that
protects the body from invaders, the translation
of sensory input into nerve impulses that are
sent to the brain, decoded there, and reassembled
into a coherent inner picture of outer reality. All
these, as well as thousands of other simultaneously
occurring functions, are coordinated perfectly by
that intelligence.
You don't run your body. Intelligence does.
It also is in charge of the organism's responses
to its environment.

Eckhart Tolle

…how immense is the raw energy pent in man
and how, if it is denied creative expression, it
will destroy both the mind which fails to find
that expression, and also the body which
attempts to give it an outlet.

Gerald Heard

83

They'll say they have fallen ill. But you don't
fall ill; you slide. Sometimes very slowly, over
a long period of abuse and lack of awareness.

Thérèse Bertherat, Carol Bernstein

Well-being cannot be infused intravenously or
ladled in by prescription. It comes from a matrix:
the bodymind. It reflects psychological and
somatic harmony.
As one anatomist put it, 'The healer inside us
is the wisest, most complex, integrated entity
in the universe.' In a sense, we know now,
there is always a doctor in the house.
'You can't deliver holistic health,'
one practitioner said. It originates in an attitude:
an acceptance of life's uncertainties,
a willingness to accept responsibility for habits,
a way of perceiving and dealing with stress,
more satisfying human relationships,
a sense of purpose.

Marilyn Ferguson

As a therapist, my first clue to this large drama
that plays out in the theater of our lives is found
in the nature and dynamics of the symptom;
thereafter, our joint task is to track the symptom
or pattern to its origin.
There is always a 'logical' connection between
a surface symptom or pattern and an historic
wounding to the soul.

James Hollis

The right reaction to a symptom may as well be
a welcoming rather than laments and demands
for remedies, for the symptom is the first herald
of an awakening psyche which will not tolerate
any more abuse.
Through the symptom, the psyche demands
attention. Attention means attending to,
tending, a certain tender care of, as well
as waiting, pausing, listening.
It takes a span of time and a tension of patience.
Precisely what each symptom needs is time and
tender care and attention. Just this same attitude
is what the soul needs in order to be felt
and heard.

James Hillman

In many cases in psychiatry, the patient who
comes to us has a story that is not told, and
which as a rule no one knows of.
To my mind, therapy only really begins after
the investigation of that wholly personal story.
It is the patient's secret, the rock against which
he is shattered.
If I know his secret story, I have a key to the
treatment. (I)n therapy, the problem is always
the whole person, never the symptom
alone – a personality, a life history, a pattern
of hopes and desires lie behind the psychosis.
Voices are now heard which demand
the treatment of the sick person, and not of
the illness. The same demand is forced upon us
in the treatment of psychic suffering. More and
more we turn our attention from the visible
disease and direct it upon the man as a whole.
We have come to understand that psychic
suffering is not a definitely localized, sharply
delimited phenomenon, but rather the symptom
of a wrong attitude assumed by the total
personality. We can therefore not hope for
a thorough cure to result from a treatment
restricted to the trouble itself, but only from
a treatment of the personality as a whole.

Carl Jung

We discovered that people experienced healing
through telling their stories.
The process opened wounds that were festering.
We cleansed them, poured ointment on them,
and knew they would heal.
A young man who had been blinded by police
action in his township came to tell us the story
of that event. When he finished he was asked
how he felt now, and he said,
'You have given me back my eyes'.

Desmond Tutu

Rehabilitation is finding a healing milieu that
offers compassionate presence, critical questioning
and insight, and steady encouragement.
It is finding a new habitat, a safe space,
a healing circle in which to explore the
sources of disintegration within oneself,
then to negotiate new health.
The circle helps its members learn to attain new
depths of self-understanding. The circle comforts
and challenges. The circle shares a wisdom quest
to find sobriety, balance, meaning, integrity.

Stephen K. Sims

Ready am I to go,
and my eagerness
with sails full set
awaits the wind.
Kahlil Gibran

The adventure that the hero is
ready for is the one he gets.
Joseph Campbell

'To be ready' has never seemed
to mean anything to me but this:
'to be straining forward'.
Teilhard de Chardin

To hope is to risk frustration.
Therefore, make up your mind
to risk frustration.
Do not be one of those who,
rather than risk failure,
never attempts anything.

Thomas Merton

And remember, too, you can stay
at home, safe in familiar illusion
of certainty.
Do not set out without realizing
that 'the way is not without danger.
Everything good is costly, and
the development of the personality
is one of the most costly of all things.'
It will cost you your innocence,
your illusions, your certainty.

Sheldon B. Kopp

One should be prepared at all times
to review one's life and to start over again
in a different place.

Etty Hillesum

The catalyst for change is the awareness
that I'm in a really tough situation,
but I've got to deal with it. It is just being
aware that you're really, really stuck.
There may be a kind of blindness for a long
time, as well as a lot of doubt, and the fear
of not really wanting to face the struggle
at all.
Then comes a readiness to face the struggle
with a sense that this is exactly what life
is all about, being ready to struggle and
make something of it.

Andrew Baumberg

The program of the soul will seldom
be found in flight, but rather in places
of spiritual risk and psychic danger
– all in service to larger life.

James Hollis

When you force solutions on problems, you
only create new problems. But when you put
your attention on the uncertainty, and you
witness the uncertainty while you expectantly
wait for the solution to emerge out of the
chaos and the confusion, then what emerges
is something very fabulous and exciting.
The state of alertness – your preparedness in
the present, in the field of uncertainty – meets
with your goal and your intention and allows
you to seize the opportunity.
What's the opportunity? It's contained within
every problem that you have in your life. Every
single problem that you have in your life is the
seed of an opportunity for some greater benefit.
Once you have that perception, you open up to
a whole range of possibilities – and this keeps
the mystery, the wonder, the excitement,
the adventure alive.

Deepak Chopra

Contact with your creative power and
its expression is related to the permission
that you give yourself to become yourself.
Nothing will happen without your permission.
Such is the power of your freedom.

Guy Corneau

The meaning is very clear; it is the meaning
of all religious practice. The individual, through
prolonged psychological disciplines, gives up
completely all attachment to his personal
limitations, idiosyncrasies, hopes and fears,
no longer resists the self-annihilation that is
prerequisite to rebirth in the realization of truth,
and so becomes ripe, at last,
for the great at-one-ment.
His personal ambitions being totally dissolved,
he no longer tries to live but willingly
relaxes to whatever may come to pass in him;
he becomes, that is to say, an anonymity.
The law lives in him with his unreserved consent.

Joseph Campbell

If you try to dislodge a nut
from its shell
when it's not ripe,
it gets very messy;
but when ripe, the slightest tap will do.

anonymous

We do not know ourselves very well;
we cannot chart the future;
we cannot control our environment completely
or the influences that work on us;
we cannot explore our unconscious
and preconscious mechanisms.
Our course is in the night;
our control is only rough and approximate;
we have to believe and trust, to risk and dare.

Bernard Lonergan

You can't cross a chasm with two leaps.

anonymous

Each of us is brought to the cliff's edge.
At such moments we can either back away
in bitterness or confusion,
or leap forward into mystery.
And what does mystery ask of us?
Only that we be in its presence,
that we fully, consciously, hand ourselves over.
That is all, and that is everything.

Philip Simmons

Be fearless,
be brave,
be bold, love yourself.

Haruki Murakami

May my mind come alive today
To the invisible geography
That invites me to new frontiers,
to break the dead shell of yesterdays,
To risk being disturbed and changed.
May I have the courage today
To live the life that I would love,
To postpone my dream no longer
But do at last what I came here for
And waste my heart on fear no more.

—

Courage is amazing because it can tap
into the heart of fear, taking that
frightened energy and turning it towards
initiative, creativity, action and hope.
When courage comes alive, imprisoning
walls become frontiers of new possibility,
difficulty becomes invitation and the heart
comes into a new rhythm of trust and sureness.
There are secret sources of courage
inside every human heart; yet courage
needs to be awakened in us.

John O'Donohue

Dare to declare who you are.
It is not far from the shores of silence
to the boundaries of speech.
The path is not long, but the way is deep.
You must not only walk there,
you must be prepared to leap.

Hildegard of Bingen

We must substitute courage for caution.

Martin Luther King

Non-violence is not a cover for cowardice,
but it is the supreme virtue of the brave.
Cowardice is wholly inconsistent
with non-violence.

Mahatma Gandhi

They [King Arthur's knights] moved out
of the society that would have protected them,
and into the dark forest, into the world of fire,
of original experience.
Original experience has not been interpreted
for you, and so you've got to work out your life
for yourself.
Either you can take it or you can't.
You don't have to go far off the interpreted path
to find yourself in difficult situations.
The courage to face the trials and to bring
a whole new field of possibilities into the field
of interpreted experience for other people
to experience – that is the hero's deed.

Joseph Campbell

What I can make conscious, face directly
and deal with as an adult, frees me from
unconscious bondage to the past.
We truly perceive that something is more
important than what we fear. And there is.
We are more important than what we fear.
This is what is meant by courage.

James Hollis

Courage, whatever else it might be, is the
capacity to resist the temptation to demand
security, certitude, or perfection
– the capacity to face uncertain and
ambiguous reality in which action
requires risk. It is apparent that these
moments of risk are moments of potential
growth and enrichment.

James Wilkes

When you become comfortable with uncertainty,
infinite possibilities open up in your life.
It means fear is no longer a dominant factor
in what you do and no longer prevents you
from taking action to initiate change.
The Roman philosopher Tacitus rightly observed
that 'the desire for safety stands against every
great and noble enterprise.'
If uncertainty is unacceptable to you, it turns
into fear. If it is perfectly acceptable, it turns into
increased aliveness, alertness, and creativity.

Eckhart Tolle

We are each of us given a quantum of energy
at birth and we have one task to perform:
identify who we are.
The most essential task of our life is to stand
up and say who we are. This is a fantastic
power we've been given.
We are given the power to create ourselves,
the same power that created stars, the same
power that created galaxies; that's the power
that's invested in us.

—

To say who we are is to say and to be someone
who has never existed before and will never
exist again. That's what differentiation means.

—

Differentiation is a task that has intrinsic
loneliness involved with it, and we shrink from
that. There's a kind of inability to stand out in
the clearing of the world and say:
'Here I am'…tremendous strength is needed
and tremendous courage to be who we are.

Brian Swimme

There is no favourable wind
for someone who does not know
where they are going.

Seneca

Focusing with perfect discipline on friendliness,
compassion, delight, and equanimity,
one is imbued with their energies.

Chip Hartranft

Inherent in every intention and desire
is the mechanics for its fulfillment...intention
and desire in the field of pure potentiality
have infinite organizing power.

Deepak Chopra

And the good, the *telos* of the intentional search,
is to be understood as a process, at once
individual and social, that is engaged in freedom,
and that consists in the making of humanity, and
its advance in authenticity, in the fulfillment of
its affectivity, and in the direction of human labor
toward cultural, social, and vital values that
are really worthwhile.

Robert M. Doran

Your life has an inner purpose and an outer purpose.
Inner purpose concerns Being and is primary.
Outer purpose concerns doing and is secondary.
…Your inner purpose is to awaken. It is as simple
as that. You share that purpose with every other
person on the planet – because it is the purpose
of humanity. Your inner purpose is an essential
part of the purpose of the whole, the universe and
its emerging intelligence.
Your outer purpose can change over time. It varies
greatly from person to person. Finding and living in
alignment with the inner purpose is the foundation
for fulfilling your outer purpose.

Eckhart Tolle

The human organism unfolds in the course of its
growth toward maturity as an acorn becomes a tree.
It moves unknowingly, and yet with a significant
development of consciousness along the way,
toward a purpose that is inherent in its nature,
a purpose contained in the seed of what it is its
nature to become.
…Wholeness is not given to man complete and
final. It is given to him rather as a possibility, as
something that can become an actuality if it
is able to grow and fulfill itself. The essence of
depth then is growth, growth toward wholeness.

Ira Progoff

When you see both particle sides, pleasure and
pain equally, the light bulb turns on.
…When you want only the positive and keep
pushing away the negative, you can't get the coin.
Most of us spend our lives trying to run from pain
and seek pleasure, instead of embracing both
in the pursuit of fulfilling our purpose.
—
Maximal evolution occurs at the border between
attraction and repulsion, pleasure and pain, order
and chaos, like and dislike.
—
When we love, we step into the full quantum
state, we align ourselves with the forces of life,
and the power of the whole universe
is suddenly behind us.

John F. Demartini

The temptation to live on the surface of life
is clear enough.
When we are pulled deeply into something,
even love, it hurts and opens us up to great
suffering.
But the willingness to open to depth is
the chief way in which dignity and purpose
return to life.

James Hollis

Another essential energy for our creativity is
the feeling of a total commissioning for this work
from the universe – that is our ground, that is
our support, a deeply felt awareness that this
creativity is needed, useful, demanded.
If you can discover who is hungry for your
creativity, you can enter into a commissioning
of your creativity; and it has to be an intuition
at a deep level that what you have to give birth
to is what is being asked for and hungered for,
even if it isn't articulated.

Brian Swimme

We withdraw from more ordinary ways
of living to devote ourselves
to a moral pursuit of goodness,
a philosophic pursuit of truth,
a scientific pursuit of understanding,
an artistic pursuit of beauty.
It is a conscious intending, ever going beyond
what happens to be given or known,
ever striving for a fuller and richer apprehension
of the yet unknown or incompletely known
totality, whole, universe.

Bernard Lonergan

Life is an energy-process.
Like every energy-process, it is in principle
irreversible and is therefore directed towards
a goal. That goal is a state of rest.
All energy-flow is like a runner who strives with
the greatest effort and the utmost expenditure
of strength to reach his goal.
Youthful longing for the world and for life,
for the attainment of high hopes and distant goals,
is life's obvious teleological urge which at once
changes into fear of life, neurotic resistances,
depression, and phobias if at some point it
remains caught in the past, or shrinks from risks
without which the unseen goal cannot be attained.
With the attainment of maturity and at the zenith
of biological existence, life's drive towards a goal
in no wise halts. With the same intensity and
irresistibility with which it strove upward before
middle age, life now descends; for the goal no
longer lies on the summit, but in the valley where
the ascent began.
The curve of life is like the parabola of a projectile
which, disturbed from its initial state of rest, rises
and then returns to a state of repose.

Carl Jung

Integrity and intention walk hand in hand.
To live intentionally is to surrender to a vision
of what one's life might become when one
allows the blind, narrow, ego-made world to
yield to an expanded truth of meaning.
Then, one's life purpose moves its focus from
the private to the common good, where pride
of personal achievement gives way to an
outward generosity of spirit.
Intentional practices of wisdom, compassion,
kindness, equanimity, and gratitude help create
a world that does not yet exist.
Personal integrity is based upon choosing
how we want to live, and designing
environments that support and strengthen
our power of intention.

Stephen K. Sims

Your life has been charted—mapped in such
a way to render the uniqueness that only you
possess.
Your purpose is to live and identify this gift,
which will, if accomplished, result in sublime
happiness and purpose. Love is the key to a
life of adventure that lies before you.
Don't miss the opportunity. You are unique.
Listen and act upon your heart.
Free your spirit. Share your gift with others.

Wayne Carroll

And you?
When will you begin
That long journey
Into yourself?

Jalal al-Din Rumi

The primary atmosphere in which the human being
moves and lives and has his being is inward.
It is contained in the way in which a person thinks
about himself, perceives and experiences
his fundamental human nature.
It involves his conception of himself, his
potentialities, and the resources upon which
he can draw.
These comprise the atmosphere of his life,
and they are within him.

Ira Progoff

(I)nstead of passing outward, beyond
the confines of the visible world, the hero
goes inward to be born again.

Joseph Campbell

The experience of emptiness, on the personal
and psychological level, introduces one to the
consciousness of what one is not, of the great,
gaping hole inside oneself, the pain of isolation,
the yearning for a wholeness of self and
relatedness with others, and the gap between
one's own possibilities and one's actual reality.
So the religious quest is a search for
wholeness, for the manifestation of one's true
self, and, at the same time, for a rootedness in
that which transcends the personal self.

Robert Jingen Gunn

Leaving the zone of everyday occupations and
relationships where everything seems clear,
I went down into my inmost self, to the deep
abyss. ...But as I moved further and further
from conventional certainties, I became aware
that I was losing contact with myself. At each
step of the descent a new person was disclosed
within me of whose name I was no longer sure,
and who no longer obeyed me. And when I had
to stop my exploration because the path faded
beneath my steps, I found a bottomless abyss
at my feet, and out it came – arising I know not
whence – the current I dare to call my life.

Teilhard de Chardin

The inner life portrays itself very accurately;
that is its most fundamental characteristic.
…It is concerned about the quality and
direction of one's life. It readily portrays
the individual's overall goals and direction.
It is even able to suggest how an individual
can get out of what binds him.
The individual feels free and acts more free
when one accurately represents one's inner
tendencies…embodies one's inner trends.
That degree of freedom diminishes as one
goes against the inner trends…the inner
is the real substance and nature of our lives.
We simply are not free to turn against it.
The inner process is exceedingly tolerant
of any effort to understand it. It can issue
forth dreams, fantasies, images forever
until you understand that which is the basis
of your understanding.

Wilson Van Dusen

When these deeper layers are opened up the
individual discovers that the unconscious world
is not just a blank abyss but that it is filled with
images and that an inner drama is proceeding,
of which he was formerly completely unaware.
If he then starts to observe these happenings
and to pay attention to them, they begin to move
and to unfold, as it were, and his inner
experiences and the pictures which image them
take on an ordered form and begin to progress
toward an unseen goal, which always carries
an aura of great value.
These experiences are uniquely individual,
arising in the secret places of one seeker's
subjective life, yet they tally in a remarkable way
with the incidents of myth and ritual, and with
the experiences of religious seekers of many
faiths and disciplines.
The habit of introversion…has been discarded,
so that for most people there is no longer
a daily renewal of contact with the inner life
which alone can safeguard the individual from
falling a victim to the natural leveling process
of the running down of energy, whose results
are only too evident today.

M. Esther Harding

Few people come to counseling who are not
driven to do so by some injury – others, who
can maintain the illusion of self-sufficiency,
will avoid contact with the inner world.
They are too content and absorbed with outer
things to pay attention to inner things.
But those who first come to the inner world
because they are forced to do so often remain
to enjoy the feast. Though they are first motivated
by some injury or failure in life, they may, through
their contact with the inner world, not only be
healed but also find the springs of creative living.

John A. Sanford

All the teachings and training in Buddhism are
aimed at that one single point: to look into the
nature of the mind, and so free us from the fear
of death and help us realize the truth of life.
Looking in will require of us great subtlety and
great courage – nothing less than a complete
shift in our attitude to life and to the mind.
We are so addicted to looking outside ourselves
that we have lost access to our inner being
almost completely. We are terrified to look inward,
because our culture has given us no idea of what
we will find. We may even think that if we do we
will be in danger of madness. This is one of the last
and most resourceful ploys of ego to prevent
us discovering our real nature.

Sogyal Rinpoche

A beggar had been sitting by the side of a road
for over thirty years.
One day a stranger walked by.
'Spare some change?' mumbled the beggar,
mechanically holding out his old baseball cap.
'I have nothing to give you,' said the stranger.
Then he asked: 'What's that you are sitting on?'
'Nothing,' replied the beggar.
'Just an old box. I have been sitting on it for as
long as I can remember.'
'Ever looked inside?' asked the stranger.
'No,' said the beggar. 'What's the point?
There's nothing in there.'
'Have a look inside,' insisted the stranger.
The beggar managed to pry open the lid. With
astonishment, disbelief, and elation, he saw
that the box was filled with gold.
I am that stranger who has nothing to give you
and who is telling you to look inside. Not inside
any box, as in the parable, but somewhere even
closer: inside yourself.
'But I am not a beggar,' I can hear you say.
Those who have not found their true wealth,
which is the radiant joy of Being and the deep,
unshakable peace that comes with it, are
beggars, even if they have great material wealth.
They are looking outside for scraps of pleasure
or fulfillment, for validation, security, or love,
while they have a treasure within that not only
includes all those things but is infinitely greater
than anything the world offers.

Eckhart Tolle

A man's work is nothing but this slow trek
to rediscover through the detours of art
those two or three great images in whose
presence his heart first opened.

Albert Camus

Freedom presupposes his imaginative powers
to conceive of the world as different from
what it is, and to conceive of himself as
different from how he is

John Douglas Mullen

Ideas and mental images shape the passion,
the movement, the direction of our lives.
From moment to moment, the choices we make
are driven by the pictures that capture
the heart and imagination.

Stephen K. Sims

Logic gets you from A to B.
Imagination will take you everywhere.

Albert Einstein

Logic and language will get us only so far.
A one-sided emphasis on hard knowledge
has diluted mystery and meaning.

Stephen K. Sims

My future is determined by me
as a working out of the relationship between
possibility and necessity. This creates for me,
as a person trying to create a future,
a constant series of existential paradoxes.
To live only in necessity is to live
as if I am what I am and can be no different.
To live only in possibility is to live
as if I can be whatever I imagine.
The problem is to hold together
a synthesis of the pair.

John Douglas Mullen

The fundamental job of the imagination in ordinary
life, then, is to produce, out of the society we have
to live in, a vision of the society we want to live in.
…We use our imagination all the time: it comes
into our conversation and practical life: it even
produces dreams when we're asleep.
Consequently we have only the choice between a
badly trained imagination and a well-trained one.
The society around us looks like the real world, but
we've just seen that there's a great deal of illusion
in it, the kind of illusion that propaganda and
slanted news and prejudice and a great deal of
advertising appeal to.
…And just as it looks real, so this ideal world that
our imaginations develop inside us looks like a
dream that came out of nowhere, and has no reality
except what we put into it.
But it isn't. It's the real world, the real form of
human society hidden behind the one we see.
It's the world of what humanity has done, and
therefore can do,
the world revealed to us in the arts and sciences…
only the cultural environment, the world we study
in the arts and sciences, can provide the kinds
of standards and values we need if we're to do
anything better than adjust…

Let us suppose that some intelligent man has been
chasing status symbols all his life, until suddenly the
bottom falls out of his world and he sees no reason
for going on. He can't make his solid gold cadillac
represent his success, or his reputation or sexual
potency anymore: now it seems to him only absurd
and a little pathetic. No psychiatrist or clergyman
can do him any good, because his state of mind is
neither sick nor sinful: he's wrestling with his angel.
He discovers immediately that he wants more
education, and he wants it in the same way
that a starving man wants food.
And no mentally healthy man wants to be a parasite:
he wants to feel he has some function, something
to contribute to the world, something that would
make the world poorer if he weren't in it.
But as soon as that notion dawns in the mind,
the world we live in, and the world we want to
live in, become different worlds.
One is around us, the other is a vision inside
our minds, born and fostered by the imagination,
yet real enough for us to try to make the world
we see conform to its shape.
This second world is the world we want
to live in, but the word 'want' is now appealing
to something impersonal and unselfish in us.

Northrop Frye

The imagination awakens the wildness of the heart.
…Social convention domesticates and controls us;
it also imprints deeply on the interior life and
would turn our one adventure in the universe
into a program of patterned social expectation.
We rarely break free; indeed, we are generally not
conscious of how smoothly we slide along the
rails of social ordering.
The awakened imagination desists from this
domestication. It returns us to our native
wildness, to the natural and seamless fluency
of our own nature.
Other worlds come into view and we are invited to
risk new and original ways of dwelling in the world.
The imagination has no patience with repetition.
The old cliches of explanation and meaning are
unmasked and their trite transparency no longer
offers shelter.
We become interested in what might be rather
than what has always been. Experimentation,
adventure and innovation lure us towards new
horizons. What we never thought possible now
becomes an urgent and exciting pathway.

John O'Donohue

We cannot quantify relationships, connectedness, transformation. Nothing in the scientific method can cope with the richness and complexity of qualitative shifts. In a transformative universe, history is instructive, but not necessarily predictive. As individuals, we are foolish if we set limits on our own or other people's potential based on past and present knowledge, including old science. For those willing to listen, science itself is telling thrilling, open-ended mystery stories about a world rich beyond our imagining. Just as one who makes a clearing in the forest is increasing the periphery of contact with the unknown, we are only becoming wiser about the scope of the territory we have yet to explore.

Marilyn Ferguson

May God give you the power
for your hidden self to grow strong
...glory be to God
whose power working in us,
can do infinitely more than
we can ask or imagine.

Ephesians 3:16,20

It would not be too much to say that myth
is the secret opening through which
the inexhaustible energies of the cosmos
pour into human cultural manifestation.
Religions, philosophies, arts, the social forms
of primitive and historic man, prime
discoveries in science and technology, the
very dreams that blister sleep, boil up from
the basic, magic ring of myth.

Joseph Campbell

The symbolic life in some form is a
prerequisite for psychic health. Without it
the ego is alienated from its suprapersonal
source and falls victim to a kind of cosmic
anxiety.
The symbol leads us to the missing part of
the whole man. It relates us to our original
totality. It heals our split, our alienation from
life. And since the whole man is a great deal
more than the ego, it relates us to the
suprapersonal forces which are the source
of our being and our meaning.
This is the reason for honoring subjectivity
and cultivating the symbolic life.

Edward F. Edinger

Myths are metaphors, and analogies, stories
that get at the heart of human behavior,
at profound truth, universal themes, ageless
patterns. They are, perhaps above all, stories
of transformation:
from chaos to form, sleep to awakening,
woundedness to wholeness, folly to wisdom,
from being lost to finding our way.
They describe the stages of life, the initiations
we all go through as we move from one level
to another: child to adult, young to old,
single to married, cowardly to courageous,
life to death, death to light.

Gregg Levoy

The meanings supplied by the organic psyche are
not intellectual creations; nor can they be described
as mainly feelings or emotions. Their essence is
the image-making faculty of the psyche; they are
products of imagination, but this is far from idle,
irrelevant fantasizing.
The meanings that arise out of the organic psyche,
often in symbolic forms, come rather from the very
nature of the human organism, very much as the
urge to build a nest arises out of the organic nature
of the hummingbird.

Ira Progoff

Archetypes are universal and timeless, depicting
the overarching patterns of human experience
– the underlying spiritual themes of human life
are everywhere the same. The same truths are
revealed through various symbolic images, truths
bigger than any particular geography, cultural
tradition, or historical moment.
Archetypes have motives that are common and
constant. They are not created by the individual
or any particular cultural tradition, but are, as it
were, spiritually organic.
They enter by way of mythic symbols, storytelling,
dream personifications, or by way of direct
experience. Taking us beyond the mundane,
spiritual archetypes guide us towards the vision
of our own creative fulfillment.
I think of archetypes as the songs of the spirit
that I hear deep inside myself. Archetypes describe
the energies of life pouring through us:
the wisdom, creativity, bliss, talent, and beauty
that bubble up from within. These energies are
activated if we listen to their inner melodies calling
us to authentic life. Archetypes point to wonder,
to where the mystery of life wants to take us. They
indicate life's profound spiritual orientations…

We ride the world of matter and spirit on a river
of images. The archetypes representing patterns
of symbolic imagery, spark spiritual imagination
to guide our development.
The symbols springing up from the unconscious
disrupt the orderly world of rational definition.
They are dynamic and have a rather unpredictable
quality. Beyond conceptual thinking, symbolic
understanding leads us into the expansive
unmapped territory of the non-rational, a world
of chaos, ambiguity, and paradox. Introducing
both disorder and transformation, symbols take
us to the edge of certainty. Our lives are hidden
in obscure mystery.
Often, when the journey that connects us to our
personal power is initiated, a powerful symbol
or metaphor will appear – that releases vitality
and points the way towards one's authentic path.
Images arise from different stratums of
the unconscious – from dreams, buried emotions,
and deep inner intelligence. As we nourish
imagination, we move closer to our true essence,
and progressively are able to affirm our boundless
possibilities.

Stephen K. Sims

The psyche of man is always full of images in a great
variety of forms, ranging from highly conscious
clarity to a blurred obscurity of meaning. These
images are highly fluid and variable. There seems to
be taking place at the several subliminal levels of the
psyche a constant flow of imagery. Included in this
are mental images, symbolic representations,
metamorphic figures, pictures, ideas, and concepts.
All these participate in a continuous flow of imagery
that underlies the production of consciousness.

Ira Progoff

Where the inherited symbols have been touched
by a Lao-tse, Buddha, Zoroaster, Christ, or
Muhammad – employed by a consummate master
of the spirit as a vehicle of the profoundest moral
and metaphysical instruction – obviously we are
in the presence rather of immense consciousness
than of darkness. Briefly formulated, the universal
doctrine teaches that all the visible structures of
the world – all things and beings – are the effects
of a ubiquitous power out of which they rise,
which supports and fills them during the period
of their manifestation, and back into which they
must ultimately dissolve. This is the power known to
science as *energy*, to the Melanesians as *mana*, to the
Sioux Indians as *wakonda*, the Hindus as *shakti*, and
the Christians as the *power of God*. Its manifestation
in the psyche is termed, by the psychoanalysts,
libido. And its manifestation in the cosmos is
the structure and flux of the universe itself.

Joseph Campbell

Symbols are spontaneous products of the archetypal psyche. One cannot manufacture a symbol, one can only discover it. Symbols are carriers of psychic energy. This is why it is proper to consider them as something alive. They transmit to the ego, either consciously or unconsciously, life energy which supports, guides, and motivates the individual. The archetypal psyche is constantly creating a steady stream of living symbolic imagery. But it is the symbolic image, acting as a releaser and transformer of psychic energy, which lifts the instinctive urgency to another level of meaning and humanizes, spiritualizes, and acculturates the raw animal energy. The instinct contains its own hidden meaning which is revealed only by perceiving the image that lies embedded in the instinct. To the extent that one is unaware of the symbolic dimensions of existence, one experiences the vicissitudes of life as symptoms. Symptoms are disturbing states of mind which we are unable to control and which are essentially meaningless – that is, contain no value or significance. Symptoms, in fact, are degraded symbols, degraded by the reductive fallacy of the ego. Symptoms are intolerable precisely because they are meaningless. Almost any difficulty can be borne if we can discern its meaning. It is meaninglessness which is the greatest threat to humanity.

Edward F. Edinger

The flower must shed its petals for the sake of
fruition, the fruit must drop off for the rebirth
of the tree. The child leaves the refuge of the womb
in order to achieve the further growth of body and
mind in which consists the whole of the child's life;
next, the soul has to come out of this self-contained
stage into the fuller life, which has varied relations
with kinsmen and neighbour, together with whom
it forms a larger body; lastly comes the decline of
the body, the weakening of desire. Enriched with
its experiences, the soul now leaves the narrower life
for the universal life, to which it dedicates its
accumulated wisdom and itself enters into relations
with the Life Eternal, so that, when finally the
decaying body has come to the very end of its tether,
the soul views its breaking away quite simply and
without regret, in the expectation of its own entry
into the Infinite.

Rabindranath Tagore

In Hindi and Sanskrit, the word for a *pilgrim site*
means a ford, a crossing place, a point of transit.
People seem most inclined to take spiritual
journeys at just such points in their own lives.
These journeys are rites of passage, rituals we
enact to help us cross over into maturity of one
kind or another…. Without these rituals, without
actively honoring that we change in dramatic ways,
the passages of our lives can become impasses.

Gregg Levoy

Mythology has a great deal to do with the stages
of life – they have to do with your recognition of
the new role that you're in, the process of throwing
off the old one and coming out in the new…
The stages of human development are the same
today as they were in the ancient times. As a child,
you are brought up in a world of discipline,
of obedience, and you are dependent on others.
All this has to be transcended when you come to
maturity, so that you can live not in dependency but
with self-responsible authority. If you can't cross
that threshold, you have the basis for neuroses.

——

The so-called rites of passage, which occupy such
a prominent place in the life of a primitive society
are distinguished by formal, and usually very severe
exercises of severance, whereby the mind is radically
cut away from the attitudes, attachments, and life
patterns of the stage being left behind. Then follows
an interval of more or less extended retirement,
during which are enacted rituals designed to
introduce the life adventurer to the forms and proper
feelings of his new estate, so that when, at last, the
time has ripened for the return to the normal world,
the initiate will be as good as reborn.

Joseph Campbell

The womb offers three things to a newly forming life: a source of possibility, a source of energy to explore that possibility, and a safe place within which that exploration can take place. Whenever these three needs are met, we have a matrix. And the growth of intelligence takes place by utilizing the energy given to explore the possibilities given while standing in the safe space given by the matrix. The biological plan for the development of intelligence is based on a series of matrix formations and shifts; that is, human beings are designed to grow in intelligence by learning about, and gaining ability to interact with one source of energy, possibility, and security after another. Each matrix shift propels us into another set of unknown unpredictable experiences, which is the way intelligence grows. Each matrix shift is both a kind of birth because we move into greater possibilities and a kind of death because the old matrix must be given up in order to move into the new.

Joseph Chilton Pearce

Psychic birth, and with it the conscious distinction of the ego from the parents, takes place in the normal course of things at the age of puberty with the eruption of sexual life. The physiological change is attended by a psychic revolution. For the various bodily manifestations give such an emphasis to the ego that it often asserts itself without stint or measure. This is sometimes called the *unbearable age*.

Carl Jung

A young man must shift the centre of gravity of his life, no longer a child in his family of origin. ...He makes and tests a variety of initial choices regarding occupation, love relationships usually including marriage and family, peer relationships, values and lifestyle. The young man has two primary yet antithetical tasks: (a) he needs to explore the possibilities for adult living: to keep his options open, avoid strong commitments and maximize the alternatives. This task is reflected in the sense of adventure and wonderment, a wish to seek out all the treasures of the new world he is entering; (b) the contrasting task is to create a stable life structure...

Daniel J. Levinson

The problem in middle life, when the body has reached its climax of power and begins to decline, is to identify yourself not with the body, which is falling away, but with the consciousness of which it is a vehicle.

—

When I retired from teaching, I knew that I had to create a new way of life, and I changed my manner of thinking about my life, just in terms of that notion – moving out of the sphere of achievement into the sphere of enjoyment and appreciation and relaxing to the wonder of it all.

Joseph Campbell

Thoroughly unprepared we take the step into
the afternoon of life; worst still, we take this step
with the false presupposition that our truths and
ideals will serve us as hitherto. But we cannot
live the afternoon of life according to the program
of life's morning – for what was great in the morning
will be little at evening, and what in the morning
was true will at evening have become a lie…
Aging people should know that their lives are not
mounting and unfolding, but that an inexorable
inner process forces the contraction of life.
The afternoon of human life must also have a
significance of its own and cannot be merely
a pitiful appendage to life's morning.
The significance of the morning, undoubtedly
lies in the development of the individual, our
entrenchment in the outer world, the propagation
of our kind and the care of our children. This is the
obvious purpose of nature. But when this purpose
has been attained, and even more than attained,
shall the earning of money, and the extension of
conquests and the expansion of life go steadily on
beyond the bounds of all reason and sense?
Whoever carries over into the afternoon the
law of the morning – that is, the aims of nature –
must pay for so doing with damage to his soul
just as surely as a growing youth who tries to
salvage his childish egoism must pay for this
mistake with social failure.

Carl Jung

Sigmund Freud stresses in his writings the passages
and difficulties of the first half of the cycle of life —
those of our infancy and adolescence, when our sun
is mounting toward its zenith. C.J. Jung, on the
other hand, has emphasized the crisis of the second
portion — when, in order to advance, the shining
sphere must submit to descend and disappear, at last,
into the night-womb of the grave. The normal
symbols of our desires and fears become converted,
in this afternoon of the biography, into their
opposites; for it is then no longer life but death that
is the challenge. What is difficult to leave, then, is
not the womb but the phallus — unless, indeed, the
life-weariness has already seized the heart, when it
will be death that calls with the promise of bliss
that formerly was the lure of love.

Full circle, from the tomb of the womb to the womb
of the tomb, we come: an ambiguous, enigmatical
incursion into the world of solid matter that is soon
to melt from us, like the substance of a dream.
And, looking back at what had promised to be
our own unique, unpredictable, and dangerous
adventure, all we find in the end is such a series
of standard metamorphoses as men and women
have undergone in every quarter of the world, in
all recorded centuries, and under every odd
disguise of civilization.

Joseph Campbell

The success with which he follows this way
to freedom and full life will depend on
the intensity of his love and will;
his capacity for self-discipline,
his steadfastness and courage.
It will depend on the generosity and
completeness of his outgoing passion
for absolute beauty, absolute goodness,
and absolute truth.

Evelyn Underhill

The moment we admit to ourselves that we are less
than we might be, that we are broken,
wounded, sinful, neurotic, maladjusted, or alienated,
we necessarily begin to try to visualize the opposite
condition – ideals are the polestars that guide us on
our journey from the actual to the possible.
And heroes are the incarnation of the ideals –
the ideals made flesh and story. We need them
because they give shape to our aspirations and
put a face on our longing for wholeness.

Sam Keen

The story of a common person in an epic journey:
the path is long and treacherous; the odds are
insurmountable.
Overpowered, outwitted and outnumbered. Again
and again, mortality is questioned. Again and again
there are miraculous escapes and unexpected allies.
The hero repeatedly steps into the unknown, love
for purpose outshining fear and doubt. Vulnerable
and not weak, complying and not yielding. Armed
only with sincerity and innocence, the hero
continues, for the cause is noble.

Bhaskar Goswami

The triune dynamic of the quest is characterized
by a) leaving home, which means departing the
old ego concept, b) enduring the enlargement of
consciousness through suffering, and c) achieving
a new place, a new home from which one must
also, in time, depart. This mythic paradigm is not
only a model for individual growth, it is also
how culture's vision is enlarged.

James Hollis

There is a virtue difficult to name that marks the
lives of those who have returned from the journey
into depths of the self. If the first part of the heroic
journey is marked by an intense focus on the self –
self-exploration, self-remembering, self-analysis,
self-criticism – the second part is marked by self-
forgetting. A man who has become fully alive is no
longer a problem to himself. He has been set free
from agonizing self-consciousness and is free to
explore and participate in the world beyond the self.
A good man does not *have* empathy; he *is* empathic.
Since he has given up the illusion that he is self-
contained, he naturally flows out to others.
The result of coming to know myself – the wounds
of shame and guilt, the disappointments of love,
the unfulfilled dreams – is that I recognize the same
in others. The unavailable man is encumbered within
himself. His preoccupation may take the form of an
obsession with money, power, reputation, health,
psychoanalysis, or even his *spiritual* journey.
Whatever the form, it renders him unavailable
to give himself to others or live vibrantly. For
the unavailable man, life is a bank account and he
always calculates how he spends and gives of himself.
The available person is not encumbered by his
possessions or his self-image, and hence has
the capacity to listen and respond to the appeal
made by others on him.

Sam Keen

The standard path of the mythological adventure
of the hero is a magnification of the formula
represented in the rites of passage:
separation – initiation – return: which might
be named the nuclear unit of the monomyth.
A hero ventures forth from the world of common
day into a region of supernatural wonder:
fabulous forces are there encountered and a
decisive victory is won: the hero comes back
from this mysterious adventure with the power
to bestow boons on his fellow man.

...Finally, the Buddha sat for seven days beneath
a fourth tree enjoying still the sweetness of
liberation. Then he doubted whether his message
could be communicated, and he thought to retain
the wisdom for himself; but the god Brahma
descended from the zenith to implore that he
should become the teacher of gods and men.
The Buddha was thus persuaded to proclaim
the path. And he went back into the cities of men
where he moved among the citizens of the world,
bestowing the inestimable boon of the knowledge
of the Way.

Joseph Campbell

No one person is able to save the world,
yet each of us is called to respond to particular
challenges and bring forth unique creativity,
a special gift. Heroes are ordinary persons
who develop their talent for the sake of a love
that is bigger than themselves.
The hero is everyone, and is found everywhere:
in office or marketplace, at home, in school or
in factory. There is an endless variety of callings:
to intellectual endeavours or concerns of social
justice, to entrepreneurial or athletic achievement,
to manual trades or scientific research.
The passionate pursuit of goodness and truth,
and the practice of charity, mark out a hero path.

—

As we heed the call to live more consciously, wisdom
carries us along a hero path towards harmony.
Heroes face transformation, they meet and
overcome trials. Despite many tribulations,
they tap into an abundant source of joy – a joy
that does not keep to itself, but shares its light,
especially those who live in darkness. What
the hero intends is to awaken creativity, passion,
love, kindness.

Stephen K. Sims

You have a part that only you can play;
and your business is to play it to perfection,
instead of trying to force fortune.
Our lives are not interchangeable.
Equally by aiming too high and by falling
too low, one misses the path to the goal.
Go straight ahead, in your own way
with God for guide.

A.D. Sertillanges

Man in his detachment has realized himself
in a wider and deeper relationship with the
universe.

—

In the freedom of consciousness he realizes
the sense of his unity with his larger being,
finding fulfilment in the dedicated life of an
ever-progressive truth and ever-active love.

Rabindranath Tagore

I have arrived.
I am home.
In the here.
In the now.
I am solid.
I am free.
In the ultimate I dwell.

Thich Nhat Hanh

Your outer journey may contain a million steps;
your inner journey only has one:
the step you are taking right now.
As you become more deeply aware of this one step,
you realize that it already contains within itself
all the other steps as well as the destination.

Eckhart Tolle

The whole future lies in uncertainty;
live immediately.

Seneca

You have never been here now before! I really
mean it. Now, sitting where you are, reading
these few words. A totally new experience.
Take a moment to feel it.
Don't be fooled by your habitual, habituated way
of experiencing life, only semi-plugged-in maybe,
but most likely unaware of being. So used to being
that you don't notice it's happening anymore.
With a superficial attention we go through life
on automatic.
Waking up means one turns attention on the being
happening now and realizes how this experience
here now – this being, embodied, this having
a mind, this consciousness being experienced now
– is absolutely new, fresh, strange, mysterious,
vivid, the present moment escaping all the time,
and this moment, new also all the time.
Take a moment to feel it, to taste what it is to be
alive and conscious here now – and now – and
now.
This statement, 'you have never been here now
before' is the greatest gift I received from my first
spiritual teacher who repeated it dozens of times.
It has inspired me to wake up here now again and
again. How is it for you to be here now in this body,
with this mind the way it is experienced just now?
Be silent and listen, the answer is immediate, lived
and felt – alive and un-known before!

Pascal Auclair

The unsettling news is that we will never
reach that elsewhere of our longing as long
as we remain in this life, as long as
we remain human.
…In our desire always to be elsewhere than here,
we can lose what measure of heaven
may be ours on earth.
When our fantasies of a better life consume us,
when our memories of past hurts bind us and
fears of pending calamity drive us, we are robbed
of the only gift – the greatest gift – we can be
sure of possessing: the present moment.
We cannot summon the future,
we cannot remake the past.
The present moment is the unfinished house
in which we dwell.

Philip Simmons

Now is the only time.
How we relate to it creates the future.
…What we do accumulates;
the future is the result of what we do right now.

Pema Chodron

No longer forward nor behind
I look in hope or fear;
But, grateful, take the good I find,
The best of now and here.

John Greenleaf Whittier

Someone once told me, 'The past is history,
the future is a mystery, and this moment
is a gift. That is why this moment is called
the present.'
If you embrace the present and become one
with it, and merge with it, you will experience
a fire, a glow, a sparkle of ecstasy throbbing
in every living sentient being. As you begin
to experience this exaltation of spirit in
everything that is alive, as you become
intimate with it, joy will be born within you,
and you will drop the terrible burdens and
encumbrances of defensiveness, resentment,
and hurtfulness. Only then will you become
light-hearted, care-free, joyous, and free.

Deepak Chopra

To ask where are the people is to ask where
are the influences, the reminders that can call
us back to what we are meant to be inwardly
– to remind us that without inner presence,
our life in time will pass us by as though we
never existed.
…We know from experience that there are
moments in life – moments of great crisis,
perhaps, or sorrow, or wonder, or even terror,
or shock, or tenderness – in which a conscious
attention appears within ourselves that is
independent of our emotions, thoughts
and sensations.
It is an attention that is pure presence. It sees
what is, what is taking place within ourselves.
It sees what thoughts are proceeding,
what emotional reactions are being activated,
what physical sensations and impulses are
being triggered.
The appearance of this conscious attention
brings with it a new sense of I am, I exist.
I exist here, I exist now.

Jacob Needleman

Concentration is born from mindfulness.
Concentration has the power to break through,
to burn away the afflictions that make you suffer
and to allow joy and happiness to come in. To
stay in the present moment takes concentration.
Worries and anxiety about the future are always
there, ready to take us away.
We can see them, acknowledge them, and use
our concentration to return to the present
moment. When we have concentration, we have
a lot of energy. We won't get carried away by
visions of past suffering or fears about the future.
We dwell stably in the present moment so we
can get in touch with the wonders of life,
and generate joy and happiness.

Thich Nhat Hanh

Of time you would make a stream,
upon whose bank.
you would sit and watch it flowing.

Kahlil Gibran

Beings endowed with self-awareness
become, precisely in virtue
of that bending back upon themselves,
immediately capable of rising
into a new sphere of existence:
in truth another world is born.

Teilhard de Chardin

The aware person lives in a world
of uniqueness and variety,
of renewal and the now.

Anthony de Mello

It is not demanded of us that we always
be in the state of the heart
which grants us vision and self-mastery.
It is only demanded of us
that we know the state we are in.

Jacob Needleman

The notion of self-awareness
– is not a looking at myself
but a being with myself.
Sebastian Moore

The billions of changes occurring in our cells
are only the passing scenery of life;
behind their mask is the seer,
who represents the source of the flow
of awareness.
Everything I can possibly experience begins
and ends with awareness;
every thought or emotion that captures
my attention is a tiny fragment of awareness;
all the goals and expectations I set for myself
are organized in awareness.
What the ancient sages termed the Self can
be defined in modern psychological terms
as a continuum of awareness, and the state
known as unity consciousness is the state
where awareness is complete – the person
knows the whole continuum of himself
without masks, illusions, gaps,
and broken fragments.
Deepak Chopra

If what you attempt is not to change yourself
but to observe yourself,
to study every one of your reactions to people
and things, without judgment or condemnation
or desire to reform yourself,
your observation will be non-selective,
comprehensive, never fixed on rigid conclusions,
always open and fresh from moment to moment.
Then you will notice a marvellous thing
happening within you:
You will be flooded with the light of awareness,
you will become transparent and transformed.
Will change occur then? Oh, yes. In you and
in your surroundings.
But it will not be brought about by your cunning,
restless ego that is forever competing, comparing,
coercing, sermonizing, manipulating in its
intolerance and its ambitions, thereby creating
tension and conflict and resistance between
you and Nature – an exhausting self-defeating
process like driving with your brakes on.
Establishing relationships is possible
only between people who are aware.
People who are unaware cannot share love.
They can only exchange desires, demands,
mutual flattery, and manipulation…

See how you attempt to bring about change
– both in yourself and in others –
through the use of punishment and reward,
through discipline and control,
through sermonizing and guilt,
through greed and pride, ambition and vanity,
rather than through loving acceptance and
patience, painstaking understanding and
vigilant awareness.
But isn't awareness an effort? Not if you have
tasted it even once.
For then you will understand that awareness
is a delight, the delight of a little child moving
out in wonder to discover the world.
For even when awareness uncovers unpleasant
things in you, it always brings liberation and joy.
Then you will know that the unaware life is not
worth living, it is too full of darkness and pain.
If at first there is sluggishness in practicing
awareness, don't force yourself.
That would be an effort again. Just be aware
of your sluggishness without any judgment or
condemnation. You will then understand that
awareness involves as much effort as a lover
makes to go to his beloved, or a hungry man
makes to eat his food, or a mountaineer to get
to the top of his beloved mountain; so much
energy expended, so much hardship even, but
it isn't effort, it's fun! In other words, awareness
is an effortless activity.

Anthony de Mello

It is necessary that we be capable of giving
substance to our life; and we can do that by
learning to make contact with the dimension
of depth that is at the core of our being.
There are levels of reality within us that
are much greater than our analytical minds
can know. Nonetheless, we can make them
accessible to our awareness so that they
become channels by which we reconnect
ourselves to the great sources of life.
Evoking the depths of ourselves is a way to
the renewal of our humanity. It is a way, and
a method, by which we can become more
truly and fully persons and by which we can
carry ourselves beyond the subjectivity
of being merely individuals
in a self-seeking world.

Ira Progoff

The moment you start *watching the thinker*,
a higher level of consciousness becomes
activated. You then begin to realize that there
is a vast realm of intelligence beyond thought,
that thought is only a tiny aspect of that
intelligence. You also realize that all the things
that truly matter—beauty, love, creativity, joy,
inner peace—arise from beyond the mind.
You begin to awaken.

Eckhart Tolle

A practice consists of all the things we do
to cultivate awareness, manage our lives
in accordance with our priorities, deepen
our connection to our true self – and
eliminate as many of the inessentials as possible.
Practice therefore includes prayer, meditation,
study, ritual, liturgy, art, body care and ethics.
Psychotherapy and psychoanalysis are also
forms of practice that are sometimes akin
to meditation, as well as study, the study
of the self and of relationships. Non-directed
thinking and meditative writing are also forms
of practice. Practice includes everything that
we do intentionally to take care of our lives,
our degree of consciousness and the life of
the world. Most essentially, practice is
a method of orienting our lives in that larger
ground of being of which we are a part,
from which we gain not only a more cohesive
sense of self, but a clear sense of direction.

Robert Jingen Gunn

Awareness is the empowerment of action.

Stephen K. Sims

The range of what we think and do
is limited by what we fail to notice.
And because we fail to notice
that we fail to notice
there is little we can do to change
until we notice
how failing to notice
shapes our thoughts and deeds.

R.D. Laing

Sit, be still, and listen,
Because you're drunk
And we're at
The edge of the roof.

Jalal al-Din Rumi

The moment one gives close attention
to anything, even a blade of grass,
it becomes a mysterious, awesome,
indescribably magnificent world in itself.

Henry Miller

Most of us go through our waking hours
taking little notice of our thought processes:
how the mind moves, what is fears, what it
heeds, how it talks to itself, what it brushes
aside, the nature of our hunches; the feel
of our highs and lows; our misperceptions.
For the most part we eat, work, converse,
worry, hope, plan, make love, shop – all
with minimal thought about how we think.
The beginning of personal transformation is
absurdly easy. We only have to pay attention
to the flow of attention itself. Immediately
we have added a new perspective.
Mind can then observe its many moods, its
body tensions, the flux of attention, its
choices and impasses, hurting and wishing,
tasting and touching.
Anything that draws us into a mindful,
watchful state has the power to transform,
and anyone of normal intelligence can
undertake such a process. Mind, in fact,
is its own transformative vehicle, inherently
prepared to shift into new dimensions if only
we let it.
Conflict, contradiction, mixed feelings, all
the elusive material that usually swirls around
the edges of awareness, can be reordered
at higher and higher levels.

Marilyn Ferguson

Most of us are not usually paying attention to what
we actually do and say. We are not really eating when
we eat; we are not really sleeping when we sleep.
Our minds are distracted and our thoughts are
scattered. Too often we are either lamenting about
and clutching at the past, or anticipating and
fearing the future. Instead of fully inhabiting
our bodies and experiencing our experience,
we're semiconscious at best – not fully present,
barely aware.

Lama Surya Das

A tutored habit of inward attention helps us
monitor a whole gamut of subjective experience:
biological, sensual, sexual, psychological, emotional,
inspirational, ethical.
In this way we come in touch with our intrinsic
beauty and goodness, thereby awakening
a new appreciation of value and meaning.
We too meet suffering and pain, and witness
our ego in the dance of its self-assertion.
If we are open to each emerging moment,
the habit of self-observation gives us the data
of our raw experience.
We notice ourselves feeling cold, angry, lonely,
hungry, joyful, jealous, tired, blissful. We notice
our behaviors, our relationships, and the roles
we play. Exactly what is happening is always
waiting to be noticed.

Stephen K. Sims

What you resist, persists.

aphorism

Pure presence is being with your experience just
as it is. You are not trying to change what is
happening, to control or resist it.
There are things going on that you do not want to
sit with. It takes courage to sit with what is. When
you do, it loses its power over you. In fact, your
resistance to what is, is
the cause of your distress.
Sometimes you think that thinking about something
is paying attention to it and dealing with it. But this
is the thinking mind, not the awareness mind.
Suppose anger comes up in your experience,
and you ask: how am I going to take care of
my anger?
Rather than pushing it away or pulling it in, you
need to see it for what it is. When you see your
anger to the core, when you see it fully,
it no longer has power to control you.

Heather Evans

The moment you become aware of a negative
state within yourself, it does not mean you have
failed. It means that you have succeeded. Until
that awareness happens, there is identification
with inner states, and such identification is ego.
With awareness comes disidentification from
thoughts, emotions, and reactions. This is not to
be confused with denial. The thoughts, emotions,
or reactions are recognized, and in the moment of
recognizing, disidentification happens
automatically. Your sense of self, of who you are,
then undergoes a shift:
before you were the thoughts, emotions, and
reactions; now you are the awareness, the conscious
presence that witnesses those states.
The more attention you give to the past, the more
you energize it, and the more likely you are to make
a 'self' out of it. Don't misunderstand: attention
is essential, but not to the past as past.
Give attention to the present; give attention to your
behavior, to your reactions, moods, thoughts,
emotions, fears, and desires as they occur in the
present. *They are* the past in you. If you can be
present enough to watch all those things, not
critically or analytically but non-judgmentally,
then you are dealing with the past and dissolving
it through the power of your presence.

Eckhart Tolle

The learning of a new technique of attention
and making the achievement of that attention
into the co-ordinating and mastering interest
of our lives is then essential.
This clearly is necessary for a double purpose;
not only because it raises the mind to contact
with that higher degree of reality whence may
be obtained the non-violent powers, but also
because only a mind which has obtained and
can retain such an experience can have
transcended its ego.
So, without the compulsion of threat, the urge
of reward or the allurement of recognition,
it is able to work co-operatively with others.

Gerald Heard

The task of union with Reality will involve certain
stages of preparation as well as stages of attainment.
...first, the disciplining and simplifying of the
attention, which is the essence of recollection. Next,
the disciplining and simplifying of the affections and
will, the orientation of the heart; which is sometimes
called by the formidable name of purgation.
(Recollection) is in essence no more and no less than
the subjection of attention to the control of the will
– it is demanded of all who would get control of
their own mental processes – (it is) the first great
step in the education of human consciousness.

Evelyn Underhill

Wonder is the lively spiritual libido
that excites us and pushes us
towards the horizon of the infinite unknown.
We are invigorated by questions,
forever tantalized by the secrets of the universe.

Stephen K. Sims

When I am asking myself a new question,
I feel tension in my body.
I go into a chaotic space inside myself,
where there is no up and no down.
I am in an unknown place that makes me feel
very uncomfortable.
In time, out of the dark unknown, an intimation,
a spark, a word, an image appears.
It's hard, but I try to stay right there, and allow
more sparks to come up before taking any next
steps. What I am saying is that my whole
being is involved:
I feel the question, I think it, I dream it.
It is important to stay with the question,
rather than grab for an answer.
When you let the process happen, there comes
a moment when there is an opening,
a moment of clarity.

Michael Abravanel

Anyone who has been stung by the eros of
inquiry knows that it can be as transformative
as the experience of love itself.
Once one starts to question, one's life is never
the same again. For there is literally nothing that
must be accepted as it is in its givenness, nothing
we cannot ask about, nothing which can justify
its claim to be exempt from the scope of
our questioning.
Once wonder is allowed free rein, there is literally
nothing that will remain what it was before we
realized we could ask what it is.
The process of questioning transforms the
ordinary world of objects into a million universes
none of which is given and all of which
invite exploration.
So upsetting is that explosion, so disorienting are
the confusion and uncertainty it engenders, it is
not surprising that we sometimes regret the loss
of the world as it was before we became questioners.
But it is only by letting that old world die that the
world of any other, in its otherness, can be born.

Jerome A. Miller

In any conversation
the person
who asks the questions
shapes the dialogue.

Sam Keen

The transcendental field is defined not by what
man knows, not by what he can know, but by
what he can ask about; and it is only because
we can ask more questions than we can answer
that we know about the limitations of our
knowledge.

—

Genuineness – does not brush questions aside,
smother doubts, push problems down; escape
to activity, to chatter, to passive entertainment,
to sleep, to narcotics.
It confronts issues, inspects them, studies
their many aspects, works out their various
implications, contemplates their consequences
in one's own life and in the lives of others.

Bernard Lonergan

We grow in the direction of the questions we ask. For questions run in front of insights – they set a process of inquiry in motion. An open life is guided by questions that probe what we do not yet know. Sometimes, it is very hard to let the questions lead us to where they want to bring us.

Questions create disquiet, tension, conflict, instability; and they leave room for movement, for expansion, the enlargement of perception. The mysteries our questions probe are infinitely complex; yet our answers are never big enough. The knowledge we come upon stands up only so long as all our tidy explanations wear out. What we think seems clear returns to confusion, becomes stale, is no longer adequate. One's stream of insight is never sufficient to grasp the whole truth of anything. The conclusions we arrive at have but a short lifespan – they fall apart time after time, disappearing ever again into a bigger mystery beyond our smaller nets of human understanding.

Stephen K. Sims

The greatness of a great question is that it can
survive any and all answering, and still be left
standing after the debates and harangues and
rational assaults have bashed away at it.
There are no great answers, you could say, but
only great questions made greater when their
answerers are nobly defeated by the awe and
mystery of the way things are.
Great questions are a proper throne for wonder,
and there is much in our lives that needs our
wonder, and deserves it, just as we ourselves
deserve the capacity for wonder that came
to us early on but does not often
survive our education.

Stephen Jenkinson

The spiritual life of human subjects is a matter
of raising and answering questions – as the
questions for meaning, for truth, and for value
are answered, the sensitive experience of
the movement of life changes. The felt tension
of inquiry comes to rest as answers emerge
in the course of the quest.
But as the questions are brushed aside and
ignored, rejected and repudiated, the sensitive
experience of the movement of life becomes
more and more chaotic, disorganized,
unsatisfied, desperate, bizarre.

Robert M. Doran

In childhood we all asked our parents
pressing meaningful questions: "Who am I?
What will happen to me when I die?
Why do things turn out the way they do?"
Few, if any, parents provided answers that were
good enough to settle the disturbing fears that
lie behind such questions, so we stopped asking
them. But they continue to linger inside us,
burning more intensely than ever.
Having reached adulthood ourselves, we tend to
dismiss these as 'ultimate questions', a label that
makes them sound very abstract.
Actually, they are the most primary questions,
and as long as they remain unresolved, the hole
that they leave creates much more of the misery
we struggle with – physical illness, emotional
malaise, a pervasive sense of restlessness, and
a nagging lack of happiness.

Deepak Chopra

A characteristic of wisdom is that it drives toward
the concerns which lie at the center of a question.
Beginning with the everyday, it leads one to
the profound, and then back again.
Having returned to the everyday, one is in a
position to apply the lessons of the journey.
The key, then, is to speak directly and concretely
to the life of the individual as he lives it, but
to speak with wisdom.

John Douglas Mullen

If you have mindfulness, concentration,
and insight,
then every step you make on this Earth
is performing a miracle.

Thich Nhat Hanh

One moment of genuine insight dispels
aeons of ignorance and confusion.

Lama Surya Das

Knowledge is nothing but
the continually burning-up of error
to set free the light of truth.

Rabindranath Tagore

The newness consists in the quality
of consciousness that lifts human activities
beyond the animal level. Man has the powers
of discernment and judgment.He can choose
this and reject that. He can value, cherish,
exalt, and especially he can understand.
The level of awareness of which the human
psyche is capable represents a high achievement
in the scale of evolution. It is a main instrument
in the growth of civilization and
in the development of the advanced capacities
of consciousness that are the fulfillment
of human personality.

Ira Progoff

The only way to make the right decision
isto know what the wrong decision is.

Paulo Coelho

Some people will never learn anything,
for this reason, because
they understand everything too soon.

Alexander Pope

A creative process is a learning process. It is
learning what hitherto was not known.
While it can take a series of disasters to convince
people of the need for creating, still the long,
hard, uphill climb is the creative process itself.
The creative task is to find the answers.
It is a matter of insight, not of one insight but
of many, not of isolated insights but of insights
that coalesce, that complement and correct one
another, that influence policies and programs,
that reveal their shortcomings in their concrete
results, that give rise to further correcting insights,
corrected policies, corrected programs, that
gradually accumulate into the all-round, balanced,
smoothly functioning system that from the start
was needed but at the start was not yet known.

Bernard Lonergan

Insight into insight brings to light the cumulative
process of progress.
For concrete situations give rise to insights
which issue into policies and courses of action.
Action transforms the existing situation to give
rise to further insights, better policies, more
effective courses of action.
It follows that if insight occurs, it keeps recurring,
and at each recurrence knowledge develops,
action increases its scope, and situations improve.

Bernard Lonergan

Self-awareness is insight. Such persons with little
of it are repressed and not insightful.
They are difficult to deal with as persons. Persons
with greater insight are easier to deal with in depth.
They have rich moment-to-moment impressions.
There is no defensive hiding. They are available
to themselves and to others.

Wilson Van Dusen

The task of consciousness always calls for critical
discernment. Whatever knowledge we glean
from our bodies, emotions, intuitions, dreams,
and revelations begs us to take pause. What we
think we *know* only approximates the truth.
The many paths by which we come to *know*
reveal partial truth, never allowing us
a complete grasp of insight.
Whether through left or right brain functioning;
or through the net of logic and language,
or intuitive grasps of meaning; or through
reasoned propositions, artistic imagination, or
sudden gestalts of understanding, our knowing
is subject to self-deception and bias.
Too, on the spiritual plane, we must discern
holy spirits from evil ones, and root out false
claims on God's will.
As we unmask the illusion and deceptions
that slant our interpretations, we let a truer
light break through.

Stephen K. Sims

Discipline is not imposed from the outside;
it is our own intelligence that must impose
it from within.
It is by using one's intelligence and by
undertaking spiritual practices where both
method and creative mental faculties are
necessary that one will learn to see the subtle
nuances between that which feeds the ego,
a function of attachment, and the positive
qualities dedicated to the good of others.
Only the union between method and wisdom
can lead to the development of valid faculties
of discernment.

Dalai Lama

So from slumber, we wake to attend.
Observing lets intelligence be puzzled, and
we inquire.
Inquiry leads to the delight of insight, but
insights are a dime a dozen, so
critical reasonableness doubts, checks,
makes sure.

Bernard Lonergan

Our desire to know and our achievement
of knowledge is not an endpoint.
There is more.
Our knowing is oriented toward action:
we desire to know because we desire to act,
and act intelligently.
Our experiencing, understanding, and judging
are directed not to just what is,
but to what is to be done;
not just to knowing reality,
but to creating reality;
and creating ourselves in the process.

Walter E. Conn

Awareness guides action, and
the higher one's level of awareness,
the more noble one's actions.
What we know informs how we choose
to act–vigorous actions issue from
vigilant awareness.
When the ambitious ego takes a back seat,
reaction is replaced by action.

Stephen K. Sims

In dreams begin responsibilities.

William Butler Yates

Goodness must be joined with knowledge.
Mere goodness is of not much use.
One must retain the fine discriminating quality
which goes with spiritual courage and character.
One must know in a crucial situation
when to speak and when to be silent,
when to act and when to refrain.
Action and non-action in these circumstances
become identical instead of being contradictory.

Mahatma Gandhi

It is not how much we do,
but how much love we put into the doing.

Mother Teresa

When you are present,
when your attention is fully in the Now,
that presence will flow into and transform
what you do.
There will be quality and power in it.
You are present when what you are doing
is not primarily a means to an end
(money, prestige, winning) but fulfilling in itself,
when there is joy and aliveness in what you do.
And, of course, you cannot be present
unless you become friendly with the present
moment. That is the basis for effective action,
uncontaminated by negativity.
In any situation and in whatever you do,
your state of consciousness is the primary factor;
the situation and what you do is secondary.
Future success is dependent upon
and inseparable from the consciousness
out of which the actions emanate.
That can be either the reactive force of the ego
or the alert attention of awakened consciousness.
All truly successful action comes out of that field
of alert attention, rather than from ego and
conditioned, unconscious thinking.

Eckhart Tolle

When we are in harmony with the way
everything proceeds from everything else,
we cannot act wrongly.
For not only are we in tune with the particular
act we are doing in terms of time,
but with all of the ways in which that act
is interrelated with everything in the universe.
It is a level of awareness from which actions
are manifested that have no clinging – not
even clinging to the effects of the act.
We are not holding on anywhere. We're right
here, always in the new existential moment.
Moment to moment it's a new mind.

Ram Dass

There is an experience of the Eternal
breaking into time, which transforms
all life into a miracle of faith and action.
Unspeakable, profound, and full of glory
as an inward experience,
it is the root of concern for all creation,
the true ground of social endeavor.
This inward life and outward concern
are truly one whole, and, were it possible,
ought to be described simultaneously.

Thomas R. Kelly

Avoid half-work more than anything.
Do something, or do nothing at all.
Do ardently whatever you decide to do;
do it with your might;
and let the whole of your activity be
a series of vigorous fresh starts.
Turn to some task which is precise,
defined in its limits,
proportioned to one's strength; and then
throw oneself into it with all one's heart.

A.D. Sertillanges

We can accomplish the most difficult
things if we have determination.
We will achieve nothing, even the easiest
things, if we take a pessimistic attitude.
According to my own experience,
determination and confidence
are the key factors to success.

Dalai Lama

When we are able to live and act without
desiring the *fruit* of our actions,
we are immediately on a spiritual path.
Even though there is no desire for fruit
in performing our daily actions,
nonetheless they do yield noble fruit.
But by simply relinquishing the desire
for results, for achievement, for success,
for gain, one is able to transcend the division
between social action and spiritual action.

—

If your actions are joyful and beautiful
then they are pure.
Beauty is the touchstone.
If the action is performed with a pure heart,
then beauty appears there.
Beauty is the outcome of pure action.

Satish Kumar

You don't repress feelings,
you negotiate them.
You find out why you feel
the way you do.

Robert M. Doran

We do not conquer thirst by repressing it.

Carl Jung

Restriction means recognizing honestly that
I desire something, and deciding then that
the prosecution of this desire is not appropriate;
whereas repression means pretending to myself
that I don't have the desire.

Sebastian Moore

The inhibited person suffers from emotional
constipation. Being in good physical condition
requires internal generation, that is, that nutrients
generate energy and what's left be discarded.
Nutrients have to pass through the body regularly.
Likewise, the generation of feelings requires
continual discharging. We must let it flow.
Otherwise the psychological buildup is poisonous,
and the ulcer makes its insidious appearance.
It's because of our good manners, the etiquette
and approval of society, that we all contribute
toward this internal constipation and that
emotional hypocrisy builds up.
Such people have no feelings or desire or joy
in being alive. Some people find it difficult to get
up in the morning; others feel nervous when
they have to meet people. Facing the world head
on demands emotion in order to leave behind the
safety and confinement of the womb and to shift
from a way of life consisting of darkness and
immobility to one of risk and flow. In striving to
keep safe and removed from risk to life, the core
of the inhibiting personality suppresses the will,
all energy turns inward, and the flow
of life is blocked.

Anthony de Mello

Sometimes old feelings
Crawl back up
Whether it's
Old pain
Old sadness
Or
Old anger
It can crawl out
Of your heart
Where it can't be kept
Much longer.
                    ASB

If we become entrenched in our emotional
routines and habits of thought, we are not
in reality – the psyche then writes its own biography.
A quality of consciousness is realized only
as we free ourselves from the grip of
unconscious complexes and negative mental states.
Beyond automatic reactivity, we are
able to re-pattern experience.

                    Stephen K. Sims

The pain-body, which is the dark shadow
cast by the ego, is actually afraid of the light
of your consciousness. It is afraid of being
found out. Its survival depends on your
unconscious identification with it, as well as
on your unconscious fear of facing the pain
that lives in you. But if you don't face it, if you
don't bring the light of your consciousness
into the pain, you will be forced to relive it
again and again.

—

The moment you observe it, feel its energy
field within you, and take your attention
into it, the identification is broken. A higher
dimension of consciousness has come in.
I call it *presence*. You are now the witness
or the watcher of the pain body.

Eckhart Tolle

The person who suppresses the animal side of
one's nature may become civilized, but does so
at the expense of decreasing the motive power
for spontaneity, creativity, strong emotions,
and deep insights.
A person cuts oneself off from the wisdom
of one's instinctual nature, a wisdom that can
be more profound than any learning or culture
can provide.

Calvin S. Hall, Vernon J. Nordby

Repressed fear and resentment signal, if anything
more efficaciously than when they are openly
expressed, to the subconscious mind of the
suspicious or violent nature which we have to win.
That is why people are often more at ease with,
and more fond of a passionate, uncontrolled
nature than of one whose spontaneity has gone,
whose cheerfulness jars as hollow and calculating,
and whose control suggests not strength but how
near hysteric breakdown lies below the surface,
and how fearful has to be its repression.

Gerald Heard

Repression constricts the emotional energy that composes the complex. Eventually this energy will prove explosive, either in relatively small but frequent outbursts of unpredictable and uncontrollable expression, or in the volcanic fashion of an act of violence.

Moral renunciation, which sometimes follows upon futile attempts at repression, is a capitulation to the power of the energies that constitute the disordered complex. The person who renounces moral responsibility for his or her disordered energy begins to act out the disorder. The project of integrating these energies through some kind of direction or control is abandoned as hopeless. The redemption of the energies bound up in these complexes over which we have no power can be effected only by a healing love that meets one at the same depth as the disorder. The victimized dimension of ourselves will not be met ultimately by judgment and condemnation, but by mercy and gentleness.

If it is responded to with compassion it can slowly be dissolved, transformed, and redirected.

The alternative to repression and moral renunciation is this compassionate negotiation of the affective forces of negativity. The dissolving of rigidly autonomous complexes under the power of the gift of love is a dimension of the replacement of the heart of stone by a heart of flesh.

Robert M. Doran

A simple feeling will arise, and instead of simply
letting it be there, we panic.
We begin to weave our thoughts into a storyline,
which gives rise to bigger emotions.
Instead of just sitting in some kind of openness
with our uncomfortable feeling, we bring out
the bellows and fan away at it.
With our thoughts and emotions, we keep it
inflamed, hot; we won't let it go.

Pema Chodron

We are capable of reliving a past event over and over,
perhaps thousands of times in one lifetime.
It is this unconscious repetition that trains
the body to remember that emotional state,
equal to or better than the conscious mind does.
When the body remembers an emotion better
than the conscious mind – in other words, when
the body is the mind – that is called a habit.
What most people don't know is that when they
think about a highly-charged emotional experience,
they make the brain fire in the exact sequences and
patterns as before; they are firing and wiring their
brains to the past by reinforcing those circuits into
evermore hardwired networks. They also duplicate
the same chemicals in the brain and body
(in varying degrees) as if they were experiencing
the event again in that moment.

Joe Dispenza

The problem of mental health, then, is always
fundamentally a problem of organisms which are
crippled, cramped, or blocked in their experience.
This is what we have learned from the long
development of psychotherapy: that intellectual
insight alone is not enough for personality
change and personal freedom.
The psychotherapist talks about the need for
'emotional insight' and 'emotional catharsis',
in addition to intellectual growth. But these are
clumsy words that really obscure the main problem.
What the patient needs is to immerse himself in a
long and total growth experience. This alone gives
him the possibility of inner or *emotional* change.
When we talk about *emotional* growth we are
talking about the forward momentum of the total
organism, moving beyond its constricting problems.
This is always both cognitive and physical, a growth
of liberating perspectives of the mind, and of inner
mellowing of the body. This is one reason that
psychotherapy has such a poor record of success:
because it cannot substitute for a whole life lived.
It is not enough to *find out* the trouble one is in, or
to straighten out his confused thoughts. Once you
find what is wrong you are still saddled with the
immense task of changing your whole
organismic seating in the world.
To aim for sanity is to aim for the long
slow growth of one's powers and sensitivities
in the real world of experience.

Ernest Becker

What is a negative emotion?
An emotion that is toxic to the body and interferes
with its balance and harmonious functioning.
Fear, anxiety, anger, bearing a grudge, sadness,
hatred or intense dislike, jealousy, envy – all disrupt
the energy flow through the body, affect the heart,
the immune system, digestion, production
of hormones, and so on.
Even mainstream medicine, although it knows very
little about how the ego operates yet, is beginning
to recognize the connection between negative
emotional states and physical disease.
An emotion that does harm to the body also infects
the people you come into contact with and
indirectly, through a process of chain reaction,
countless others you never meet. There is a generic
term for all negative emotions: unhappiness.

Eckhart Tolle

Just as the well-tended compost becomes a
flower garden, when we take care of and look
deeply into our sorrow, it transforms into
understanding and compassion.
With mindfulness, the feelings that have been
painful and difficult transform into something
beautiful: the wondrous, healing balm of
understanding and compassion.

Thich Nhat Hanh

Because of the centrality of feelings in moral consciousness, this discriminating process of enriching, refining, and pruning of feelings is the heart of moral education – because self-knowledge is of the whole person, authenticity requires that we take cognizance of all our feelings.

Walter Conn

When you are focusing well, you are glad about the coming of any feeling. You might hear an inner voice say, 'You're doomed!' You would consider this gently and understandably. You would say, 'Oh that's interesting. A feeling of doom. No wonder I felt locked up – if there's been a feeling like that in there. Glad it came up. Let's find out where that feeling comes from.'
The bad feeling is the body knowing and pushing toward what good should be. Every bad feeling is potential energy toward a more right way of being if you give it space to move toward its rightness. The sense of wrong carries with it, inseparably, a sense of the direction toward what is right.
…It is important to accept every feeling that comes, not argue with it, not challenge it with peremptory demands that it explains itself. You don't talk back to the feeling – instead you approach the feeling in an accepting way.
The *problems* inside you are only those parts of the process that have been stopped, and the aim of focusing is to get the process moving again.

Eugene Gendlin

Why do some persons engage in addictions?
Because they all have deep emotional problems
they don't have the means to resolve on their own.

Gabor Maté

…It is much better to take full cognizance of one's
feelings, however deplorable they may be, than
to brush them aside, overrule them, ignore them.
It is true, of course, that fundamentally feelings are
spontaneous. They do not lie under the command
of decision – but once they have arisen, they may
be reinforced by advertence and approval, and they
may be curtailed by disapproval and distraction.
…There are too the feelings that have been snapped
off by repression to lead thereafter an unhappy
subterranean life. But there are in full consciousness
feelings so deep and strong, especially when
deliberately reinforced, that they channel attention,
shape one's horizon, direct one's life.

Bernard Lonergan

When you look at a tree in a storm, if you focus
your attention on the top of the tree,
you'll see the leaves and branches blowing wildly
in the wind, and the tree will look so vulnerable,
as though it could be broken at any time.
But when you direct your attention down to the
trunk of the tree, there's not so much movement.
You see the stability of the tree, and you see that
the tree is deeply rooted in the soil and can
withstand the storm.
When we experience a strong emotion, the mind
is agitated like the top of the tree. We have to
bring our mind down to the trunk, to the
abdomen, and focus all our attention
on the rise and fall of the abdomen.
Breathing in, you notice the rising of your abdomen.
Breathing out, notice the falling of your abdomen.
Breathe and focus your attention on your
in-breath and out-breath.
If there is anything to be aware of, it's that an
emotion is only an emotion, and that you are
much more than one emotion. You are body,
feelings, perceptions, mental formations, and
consciousness. The territory of your being is large.

Thich Nhat Hanh

The privilege of a lifetime is being who you are.
Joseph Campbell

There is a way to remain in real time with
the universe, but it is not through force,
imagination or manipulation.
It Is by finding and recognizing your true Self.
When you do, you will not need to manipulate
anything. All will be observed to be flowing
in perfect harmony.
Mooji

Be yourself; everyone else is already taken.
Oscar Wilde

This, after all is said and done, is the only real
problem of life, the only worthwhile preoccupation
of man: What is one's true talent, his secret gift,
his authentic vocation? In what way is one truly
unique, and how can he express this uniqueness,
give it form, dedicate it to something beyond
himself? How can the person take his private inner
being, the great mystery that he feels at the heart of
himself, his emotions, his yearnings and use them
to live more distinctively, to enrich both himself
and mankind with the peculiar quality of his talent?
In adolescence, most of us throb with this dilemma,
expressing it either with words and thoughts or
with simple numb pain and longing. But usually life
sucks us up into standardized activities. The social
hero-system into which we are born marks out
paths for our heroism, paths to which we conform,
to which we shape ourselves so that we can please
others, become what they expect us to be.
And instead of working our inner secret we
gradually cover it over and forget it, while we
become purely external men, playing successfully
the standardized hero-game into which we happen
to fall by accident, by family connection, by reflex
patriotism, or by the simple need to eat
and the urge to procreate.

Soren Kierkegaard

Inner intelligence lies at the heart of human
authenticity, ever pushing us in the direction
of integral growth.
We are internally organized towards a specific
purpose, and every individual has a unique
story that awaits expression.
As we bring forth our special gifts in response
to our deepest longings, each of us creates
a singular path.
True intention and true talent find each other,
and develop together.

Stephen K. Sims

There is a certain way of being human that
is my way. I am called to live my life in this way,
and not in imitation of anyone else's.
But this gives a new importance to being true
to myself. If I am not, I miss the point of my life...

Charles Taylor

...The obstacles to inner growth take different
forms, however similar they are under the surface.
Always and everywhere, the difficulties standing
in the seeker's way are more subtle than one may
think. The founding legends of spiritual traditions
– the lives of Jesus, the Buddha, the Baal Shem,
Muhammad – portray a struggle of heroic
proportions, requiring not only goodwill
but extraordinary intelligence, humility, strength
of purpose, and courage. And though the inner
struggle is never easy in a way that we might
dream of, nor difficult in the ways we might fear,
it is first and last a struggle, and principally
a struggle with oneself, with certain aspects of
our own minds, hearts, and bodies. Anyone who
has ever undertaken this struggle knows it is far
easier to speak about it than to engage in it.

Jacob Needleman

Man is a spirited being. When you say
'I like a person with spirit',
you are referring to someone who is
self-possessed, who thinks for himself,
controls his own life, refuses to be passive,
refuses to be controlled from without.

John Douglas Mullen

I don't have to prove my life.
I just have to live.

Dan Berrigan

Conversion is a change of direction, and
indeed, a change for the better. One frees
oneself from the inauthentic. One grows
in authenticity.
Harmful, dangerous, misleading satisfactions
are dropped. Fears of discomfort, pain,
privation have less power to deflect one
from one's course.
Values are apprehended when before they
were overlooked. Scales of preference shift.
Errors, rationalizations, ideologies fall
and shatter to leave one open to things
as they are and to man as he should be.

Bernard Lonergan

My life is my message.

Mahatma Gandhi

So with our soul. When the heat and motion
of blind impulses and passions distract it
on all sides, we can neither give nor receive
anything truly. But when we find our centre
in our soul by the power of self-restraint, by
the force that harmonizes all warring elements
and unifies those that are apart, then all
our isolated impressions reduce themselves
to wisdom, and all our momentary impulses
of heart find their completion in love; then all
the petty details of our life reveal an infinite
purpose, and all our thoughts and deeds unite
themselves inseparably in an internal harmony.

Rabindranath Tagore

So human authenticity is never some pure
and secure and serene possession.
It is ever a withdrawal from inauthenticity,
and every successful withdrawal only brings
to light the need for still further withdrawals.

Bernard Lonergan

You are your own greatest text. Know thyself!
You are the microcosm of the macrocosm;
when you know yourself, you know the universe.
Satish Kumar

In sooth, I know not why I am so sad,
It wearies me.
You say it wearies you?
But how I caught it, found it, or came by it
What stuff t'is made of
Whereof it is born,
I am to learn
And such a want-wit sadness makes of me,
That I have much ado to know myself.
William Shakespeare

If only a portion of that lost totality
could be dredged up into the light of day,
we should experience a marvelous expansion
of our powers, a vivid renewal of life.
Joseph Campbell

The sad truth is that we remain necessarily
strangers to ourselves, we don't understand
our own substance, we must mistake
ourselves; the axiom, "Each man is farthest
from himself" will hold for us to all eternity.
Of ourselves we are not *knowers*…

Friedrich Nietzsche

To look at oneself deeply, persistently, and
honestly takes insight and courage.
It is to attempt to see one's life as the expression
of a set of values, and to isolate and evaluate
those values.
…this kind of analysis is nothing other than
an attempt to answer the questions 'Who am I?'
and 'Am I someone of whom I can in the most
fundamental sense be proud?'
To answer these questions one must have some
insight into what genuine human life is; what
promises it holds in the optimum; what anxieties
are fundamental to it; and what kinds of things
are truly worthwhile.

John Douglas Mullen

The individual who wishes to have an answer
to the problem of evil – has need first and
foremost, of *self-knowledge*, that is the
utmost possibility of his own wholeness.
He must know relentlessly how much good he
can do, and what crimes he is capable of, and
must beware of regarding the one as real and
the other as illusion.
Both are elements within his nature, and both
are bound to come to light in him, should he
wish – to live without self-deception or
self-delusion.
Such self-knowledge is of prime importance,
because through it we approach that
fundamental stratum or core of human nature
where the instincts dwell.
Here are those pre-existent dynamic factors
which ultimately govern the ethical decisions
of our consciousness.
We achieve knowledge of nature only
through science, which enlarges consciousness;
hence deepened self-knowledge also requires
science, that is, psychology.

Carl Jung

Holiness is not an achievement, it is a grace.
A grace called *awareness*, a grace called
looking, observing, understanding.
If you would only switch on the light of awareness
and observe yourself and everything around you
throughout the day, if you would see yourself
reflected in the mirror of awareness the way you
see your face reflected in a looking glass, that is,
accurately, clearly, exactly as it is without the
slightest distortion or addition, and if you
reserved this reflection without any judgment or
condemnation, you would experience all sorts
of marvelous changes coming about in you.
Only you will not be in control of those changes,
or be able to plan them in advance, or decide
how and when they are to take place.
It is this nonjudgmental awareness alone
that heals and changes and makes one grow.
But in its own way and at its own time.

Anthony de Mello

Mystery surrounds every experience of the
human heart: the deeper we go into the heart's
darkness or its light, the closer we get to
the ultimate mystery of God.
But our culture wants to turn mysteries into
problems to be solved or breakdowns to be fixed,
because maintaining the illusion that we can
straighten things out makes us feel powerful.
Yet mysteries never yield to solutions or fixes
– and when we pretend that they do, life not only
becomes more banal but more hopeless, because
the fixes never work. Embracing the mystery of
depression does not mean passivity or resignation.
It means entering into a field of forces that
seems alien but is in fact our deepest self.
It means waiting, watching, listening, suffering,
and gathering whatever self-knowledge we can – and
then making choices based on that knowledge, no
matter how difficult. We begin the slow walk back
to health by choosing each day that which enlivens
our selfhood and resisting that which does not.

Parker Palmer

This climb up the mountain of self-knowledge…
is the necessary prelude to all illumination.
Only at its summit do we discover…
the beginning of the pathway to Reality.
It is a lonely and arduous excursion, a sufficient
test of courage and sincerity: for most men prefer
to dwell in comfortable ignorance upon the
lower slopes…
Ascending the mountain of self-knowledge and
throwing aside your superfluous baggage as you
go, you shall at last arrive at the point which they
call the summit of the spirit; where the various
forces of your character
– brute energy, keen intellect, desirous heart –
long dissipated amongst a thousand little wants
and preferences, are gathered into one, and
become a strong and disciplined instrument
wherewith your true self can force a path deeper
and deeper into the heart of Reality.

Evelyn Underhill

But to have what we seek, we have to go beyond
knowing and become it.
It is a peculiar predicament that the knowledge
can only be known by our transforming ourselves
into the knowledge itself.

Ram Dass

EPILOGUE

*We wanderers, ever seeking the lonelier
way, begin no day where we have ended
another day; and no sunrise finds us
where sunset left us.
Even while the earth sleeps we travel.
We are the seeds of the tenacious plant,
and it is in our ripeness and our fullness
of heart that we are given to the wind
and are scattered.*

—

*The river cannot go back.
No one can go back.
To go back is impossible in existence.
The river needs to take the risk of entering
the ocean because only then will fear
disappear,
because that's where the river will know
it's not about disappearing into the ocean,
but of becoming the ocean.*

                    Kahlil Gibran

The first stretch of *The Noble River* journey comes to a close. As we continue to ply the waters of the unknown, delight and gratitude abound. However, we now need to tighten the grip on our paddles – challenging whitewater lies ahead.

The voices of our river guides summon us to find and follow a path into love. They ask us to seek out and give expression to our hidden wholeness. Beyond illusion, beyond the narrow self, beyond the restless mind of ordinary consciousness lies one's essential self: timeless, infinite, still.

Wisdom asks for continuous awakening. It leads us to our growth edge and calls forth courage to work through the fears that inhibit our capacity to love.

The way of wisdom draws forth a new quality of consciousness allowing us to be who we truly are. Wisdom is that knowledge that invites us to come home to ourselves, ever instructing us to go on growing in love.

As we journey, let wisdom shine its light into our darkness. May each of us come to know the profound joy of our oneness in love.

THEME 1   WISDOM

Bernard Lonergan, *Method in Theology* (Toronto: University of Toronto Press, 1990) 77.

Chip Hartranft (translation & commentary), *The Yoga-Sutra of Patanjali* (Boulder: Shambhala, 2003) 1.

Joseph Campbell, *The Power of Myth, with Bill Moyers* (New York: Doubleday, 1988) 9, 99. (2)

Lama Surya Das, *Awakening the Buddha Within* (New York: Broadway Books, 1998) 42, 84, 96. (3)

Rabindranath Tagore, *Sadhanna* (Fairfield, IA: 1st. World Library, 2005) 30.

Ralph Waldo Emerson, *Self-Reliance* (New York: Bell Tower, Harmony Books, 1991) 44.

The Bible: Proverbs 2:1-5, 3:13-18. (2)

The Dhammapada: Juan Mascaro, trans.(London: Penguin Books, 1973) 55.

Thomas Merton, *Gandhi on Non-Violence* (New York: New Directions, 1964) 1.

THEME 2   JOURNEY

A.D. Sertillanges, *The Intellectual Life* (Netherlands: Bosch Utrecht, 1948) 41.

Dag Hammarskjöld, *Markings* (New York: Alfred A. Knopf, 1964) 5, 58, 7, 8. (4)

David Steindl-Rast, *Essential Writings* (Maryknoll, New York: Orbis Books, 2010) (ed. Clare Hallward) 71.

Eckhart Tolle, *A New Earth* (New York/Toronto: A Plume Book, Penguin Group, 2005) 271.

Gerald Heard, *Pain, Sex and Time* (Rhinebeck, NY : Monkfish Book Publishing Company, 2004 /first published 1939) 172-3.

Ira Progoff, *The Symbolic & the Real* (New York: McGraw-Hill Book Company, 1973) 213.

Kahlil Gibran, *The Prophet* (London: Penguin Group, first published 1926 / Penguin Arkana later edition, 1998) 4.

Mahatma Gandhi, *All Men Are Brothers* (UNESCO, 1958) 169.

Marilyn Ferguson, *The Aquarian Conspiracy* (Los Angeles: J.P. Tarcher, 1980) 101.

Northrop Frye, *The Educated Imagination* (The Massey Lectures — series two — Canadian Broadcasting Corporation, 1963) 4.

Sheldon B. Kopp, *If You Meet The Buddha On The Road, Kill Him* (New York: Bantam Books, 1976) 3.

Stanley Kunitz, *The Wild Braid* (New York: W.W. Norton & Company, 2007) 140.

THEME 3   CALL

Ben Okri, *Songs of Enchantment*

Brian Swimme, *The Universe Is A Green Dragon* (Santa Fe: Bear & Company, 1984) 117-8.

Dag Hammarskjöld, *Markings* (New York: Alfred A. Knopf, 1964) 205.

Gregg Levoy, *Callings*(New York: Three Rivers Press, 1997) 325.

Hermann Hesse, *Siddhartha* (New York: New Directions, 1957) 67.

Howard Thurman … source unknown

Jacob Needleman, *Time and the Soul* (San Francisco, Berrett-Koehler Publishers, 2003) 33.

James Hollis, *Finding Meaning in the Second Half of Life* (New York: Gotham Books, Penguin Group-USA Inc., 2006) 21.

John O'Donohue, *Beauty* (New York: Harper Perennial, 2005) 135.

Joseph Campbell, *The Hero With A Thousand Faces* (Princeton, New Jersey: Princeton University Press, 1972) 51.

Ralph Waldo Emerson, *Self-Reliance* (New York: Bell Tower, Harmony Books, 1991) 44-5.

Stephen K. Sims, *The Wisdom of Authenticity* (Montreal: self-published, 2015) 3.

THEME 4   LONGING / SEEKING

Brian Swimme, *The Universe Is A Green Dragon* (Santa Fe: Bear & Company, 1984) 51.

Evelyn Underhill, *Mysticism* (New York: Image Books, Doubleday, 1990 / first published 1911) 126-7.

Ira Progoff, *The Symbolic & the Real* (New York: McGraw-Hill Book Company, 1973) 215.

Jalal al-Din Rumi ... source unknown

Joseph Campbell, *The Power of Myth, with Bill Moyers* (New York: Doubleday,1988) 120.

Kabir, translator Rabindranath Tagore assisted by Evelyn Underhill, *One Hundred Poems of Kabir* (London: MacMillan and Co. Limited, 1915).

Kahlil Gibran, *The Prophet* (London: Penguin Group, first published 1926 / Penguin Arkana later edition, 1998) 73-4.

Mahatma Gandhi, *All Men Are Brothers* (UNESCO, 1958) 59.

Rabindranath Tagore, *Sadhanna* (Fairfield, IA: 1st. World Library, 2005) 48-9.

Ralph Waldo Emerson, *Self-Reliance* (New York: Bell Tower, Harmony Books, 1991) 63.

Stephen K. Sims, *The Wisdom of Authenticity* (Montreal: self-published, 2015), 7 / *River of Awareness* (first edition: Toronto, Novalis Publishing, 2009) 85-6.

Vernon Gregson, The Desires of the Human Heart (Mahwah, New Jersey: Paulist Press, 1988) 16-17.

THEME 5   AWAKENING

Diarmuid O'Murchu ... source unknown

Jalal al-Din Rumi ... source unknown

John O'Donohue, *To Bless the Space Between Us* (New York: Doubleday, 2008) 7-8.

José Ortega y Gasset, cited in Ernest Becker, *The Denial of Death* (New York: The Free Press, 1973) 89.

Kabir, translator Rabindranath Tagore assisted by Evelyn Underhill, *One Hundred Poems of Kabir* (London: MacMillan and Co. Limited, 1915).

Marilyn Ferguson, *The Aquarian Conspiracy* (Los Angeles: J.P. Tarcher, 1980) unknown / 73. (2)

Pema Chodron, When Things Fall Apart (Boston: Shambhala Classics, 2000) 121, 123. (2)

Rabindranath Tagore, *Sadhanna* (Fairfield, IA: 1st. World Library, 2005) 71-2.

Ram Dass ... source unknown

Stephen K. Sims, *The Wisdom of Authenticity* (Montreal: self-published, 2015) 66 / *River of Awareness* (first edition: Toronto, Novalis Publishing, 2009) 26.

Zen master ... source unknown

THEME 6   BECOMING

Eda LeShan, *Grandparenting in a Changing World* (Newmarket Press, 1993) 173-4.

Friedrich Nietzsche ... source unknown

Joel Goldsmith ... source unknown

John O'Donohue ... *Beauty* (New York: Harper Perennial, 2005) unknown, 146. (2)

Joseph Campbell, *The Hero With A Thousand Faces* (Princeton, New Jersey: Princeton University Press, 1972) 289.

Joseph Chilton Pearce, *Magical Child* (New York: Bantam Books, 1980) 90.

Marilyn Ferguson, *The Aquarian Conspiracy* (Los Angeles: J.P. Tarcher, 1980) 164-5.

Mary Parker Follett, a collection edited by François Héon, Albie Davis, Jennifer Jones Patulli, Sébastian Damart: *The Essential Mary Parker Follet* (Montreal: 2014) 29.

Robert Jingen Gunn, *Journeys into Emptiness* (New Jersey: Paulist Press, 2000) 280.

Sam Keen ... source unknown

Sebastian Moore ... source unknown

Stanley Kunitz, *The Wild Braid* (New York: W.W. Norton & Company, 2007) 3.

THEME 7   CHANGE

Avram Davis, *The Way of the Flame* (San Francisco: Harper Collins, 1996) 23-4.

Gerald Heard, *Pain, Sex and Time* (Rhinebeck, NY : Monkfish Book Publishing Company, 2004 / first published 1939) 178.

Henri J.M. Nouwen, 'Living in Joyful Ecstasy' in *Sojourners 14,* August-September, 1985) 27.

Heraclitus ... source unknown

Hindu proverb

Jerome A. Miller, *'The Auroral Hour and the Throe of History'* (Cross Currents, spring 1997) 64.

Jon Kabat-Zinn ... source unknown

Lama Surya Das, *Awakening the Buddha Within* (New York: Broadway Books, 1998).

Max Planck ... source unknown

Placide Gaboury, Church and Spirituality (Montreal: lecture, Loyola College, 1982) transcript page 7.

Ralph Waldo Emerson, *Self-Reliance* (New York: Bell Tower /Harmony Books, 1991) 143-4.

Stanley Kunitz, *The Wild Braid* (New York: W.W. Norton & Company, 2007) 105.

Stephen K. Sims, *River of Awareness* (first edition: Toronto, Novalis Publishing, 2009) 31 / *The Wisdom of Authenticity* (Montreal: self-published, 2015) 40. (2)

The Serenity Prayer

THEME 8   **VISION/ POTENTIAL**

Desmond Tutu, *Justice, Memory, and Reconciliation Symposium* (lecture given in Toronto: February 2000).

Epictetus ... source unknown

Gerald Heard, *Pain, Sex and Time* (Rhinebeck, NY : Monkfish Book Publishing Co, 2004; first published 1939) 263.

Haruki Murakami ... source unknown

Ira Progoff, *Depth Psychology & Modern Man* (New York: McGraw-Hill Book Company, 1973) 7.

Ira Progoff, *The Symbolic & the Real* (New York: McGraw-Hill Book Company, 1973) 59-60.

Joseph Campbell, *Reflections on the Art of Living–A Joseph Campbell Companion* (edited by Diane K. Osbon) (New York: HarperPerennial, 1991) 18.

Marilyn Ferguson, *The Aquarian Conspiracy* (Los Angeles: J.P. Tarcher, 1980) 169-70.

Martin Buber ... source unknown

Norman Cousins, forward to: Robert Muller, *Happiness* (Los Angeles: Amare Media, 2005) 10.

Parker Palmer, *Let Your Life Speak* (San Francisco: Jossey-Bass, 2000) 4.

Seth Godin ... source unknown

Stephen K. Sims, *The Wisdom of Authenticity* (Montreal: self-published, 2015) 21-2.

THEME 9   **ESSENCE**

Carl Jung, *Memories, Dreams, Reflections* (New York: Vintage books, Random House, 1989; first published 1963) 358.

Deepak Chopra, *The Seven Spiritual Laws of Success* (San Rafael, CA: Amber-Allen Publishing and New World Library, 1994) 18-19.

Eckhart Tolle, *A New Earth* (New York/Toronto: A Plume Book, Penguin Group, 2005) 220, 4. (2)

Evelyn Underhill, *Practical Mysticism* (Columbus, Ohio: Ariel Press, 1987 / first published 1914) 59-60.

Jalal al-Din Rumi ... source unknown

Lama Surya Das, *Awakening the Buddha Within* (New York: Broadway Books, 1998) 316.

Stephen K. Sims ... personal notes

Teilhard de Chardin, *The Prayer of the Universe* (New York: Collins Fountain Books, 1965) 55.

Wilson Van Dusen, *The Natural Depth in Man* (1st. edition: New York: Harper & Row, 1972) / (2nd. printing: The Swedenborg Foundation, 1981) 4, 74. (2)

THEME 10   MEANING

Carl Jung, *Memories, Dreams, Reflections* (New York: Vintage, Random House, 1989 / first published, 1963) 326, 140, 318. (3)

Carl Jung … source unknown

Ernest Becker, '*The Pawnbroker*' found in *Angel in Armour* (New York: George Braziller, 1969) 80.

Gerald Heard, *Pain, Sex and Time* (Rhinebeck, NY : Monkfish Book Publishing Company, 2004 / first published 1939) 25-6.

Gerald Heard … source unknown

Ira Progoff, *The Symbolic & the Real* (New York: McGraw-Hill Book Company, 1973) 13, 80. (2)

James Hollis, The Archetypal Imagination (Texas A&M University Press, 2000) 16.

Stephen K. Sims, *The Wisdom of Authenticity* (Montreal: self-published, 2015) 10.

Viktor E. Frankl, *Man's Search for Meaning* (New York: Washington Square Press, Pocket, 1959) 126, 131; 133-5. (3)

THEME 11   SELF-DEVELOPMENT

A.D. Sertillanges, *The Intellectual Life* (Netherlands: Bosch Utrecht, 1948) 148.

Bernard Lonergan, Insight (Toronto: University of Toronto Press, reprinted 1997) 648.

Bernard Lonergan, *Existenz and Aggioramento* (lecture, 1964) found in the *First Collection* (Toronto: University of Toronto Press, 1993) 223-4.

Dan Berrigan … source unknown

John Douglas Mullen, *Kierkegaard's Philosophy* (New York: a Mentor Book, The New American Library, Inc., 1981) 21, 26. (2)

John C. Maxwell, *How Successful People Grow.*

Joseph Chilton Pearce, *Magical Child* (New York: Bantam Books, 1980) 3.

Lama Surya Das, *Awakening the Buddha Within* (New York: Broadway Books, 1998) 6.

Marilyn Ferguson, *The Aquarian Conspiracy* (Los Angeles: J.P. Tarcher, 1980) 116.

Milton Dawes ... personal journal

Placide Gaboury, Church and Spirituality (Montreal: lecture, Loyola College, 1982) transcript 7.

Stephen K. Sims, *The Wisdom of Authenticity* (Montreal: self-published, 2015) 26.

The Talmud

THEME 12   **BODY-MIND HEALING**

Carl Jung, *Memories, Dreams, Reflections* (New York: Vintage books, Random House, 1989, first published 1963) 117, 127. (2)

Carl Jung, *Modern Man in Search of a Soul* (New York: A Harvest HBJ Book, 1933) 192.

Deepak Chopra, *Quantum Healing* (New York: Bantam Books, 1989) 106.

Desmond Tutu, *Justice, Memory, and Reconciliation Symposium* (lecture given in Toronto: February 2000).

Eckhart Tolle, *A New Earth* (New York/Toronto: A Plume Book, Penguin Group, 2005) 132.

Gerald Heard, *Pain, Sex and Time* (Rhinebeck, NY : Monkfish Book Publishing Company, 2004 / first published 1939) 117.

James Hillman, *Insearch* (Dallas: Spring Publications Inc, 1967) 56.

James Hollis, *Finding Meaning in the Second Half of Life* (New York: Gotham Books, Penguin Group-USA Inc., 2006) 20.

Kabir, translator Rabindranath Tagore assisted by Evelyn Underhill, *One Hundred Poems of Kabir* (London: MacMillan and Co. Limited, 1915).

Marilyn Ferguson, *The Aquarian Conspiracy* (Los Angeles: J.P. Tarcher, 1980) 248.

Stephen K. Sims, *River of Awareness* (first edition: Toronto, Novalis Publishing, 2009) 128.

Thérèse Bertherat and Carol Bernstein, *The Body Has Its Reasons* (Avon of Bard, Camelot, 1977) 97.

The Buddha : *Anguttara Nikaya* (cited in Wes Nisker, *Buddha's Nature* (New York: Bantam Books, 1998) 33.

THEME 13   **READINESS / RISK**

Andrew Baumberg … in conversation

Anonymous

Bernard Lonergan, *Existenz and Aggioramento* (lecture, 1964) found in the *First Collection* (Toronto: University of Toronto Press, 1993) 224.

Deepak Chopra, *The Seven Spiritual Laws of Success* (San Rafael, CA: Amber-Allen Publishing and New World Library, 1994) 89.

Etty Hillesum, *An Interrupted Life* (New York: Washington Square Press, Pocket Books, 1985) 163.

Guy Corneau … source unknown

James Hollis, *Finding Meaning in the Second Half of Life* (New York: Gotham Books, Penguin Group-USA Inc. 2006) 169.

Joseph Campbell, *The Power of Myth, with Bill Moyers* (New York: Doubleday,1988) 129.

Joseph Campbell, *The Hero With A Thousand Faces* (Princeton, New Jersey: Princeton University Press, 1972) 204-5.

Kahlil Gibran, *The Prophet* (London: Penguin Group, first published 1926 / Penguin Arkana later edition, 1998) 7.

Sheldon B. Kopp, *If You Meet The Buddha On The Road, Kill Him* (New York: Bantam Books, 1976) (quoting Richard Wilhelm) 10.

Teilhard de Chardin, *Hymn of the Universe* (New York: Collins Fontana Religious Books, 1970) 90.

Thomas Merton, *New Seeds of Contemplation* (New York: New Directions, 1972) 104.

THEME 14   **COURAGE**

Anonymous

Brian Swimme, *Canticle to the Cosmos*, video 4.

Eckhart Tolle, *A New Earth* (New York /Toronto: A Plume Book, Penguin Group, 2005) 276.

Haruki Murakami … source unknown

Hildegard of Bingen … source unknown

James Hollis, *Swamplands of the Soul* (Toronto: Inner City Books 1996) 116.

James Wilkes, *The Gift of Courage* (Toronto: The Anglican Book Centre, 1979) 28.

John O'Donohue, (1) *To Bless the Space Between Us* (New York: Doubleday, 2008) 9.

(2) *Beauty* (New York: Harper Perennial, 2005) 6.

Joseph Campbell, *The Power of Myth, with Bill Moyers* (New York: Doubleday,1988) 41.

Mahatma Gandhi (cited in Thomas Merton, Gandhi on Non-Violence (New York: New Directions, 1964) 36.

Martin Luther King Jr ... source unknown

Philip Simmons, *Learning to Fall* (N.Y.: Bantam Books, 2002) 8.

THEME 15   **INTENTION / PURPOSE**

Bernard Lonergan, *Method in Theology* (Toronto: University of Toronto Press, 1990) 13.

Brian Swimme, *Canticle to the Cosmos*, video 4, 6.

Carl Jung, cited in Jenny Yates, *Jung on Death and Immortality* (New Jersey: Princeton University Press, 1999) 12-3.

Chip Hartranft (translation & commentary), *The Yoga-Sutra of Patanjali* (Boulder: Shambhala, 2003) 52.

Deepak Chopra, *The Seven Spiritual Laws of Success* (San Rafael, CA: Amber-Allen Publishing and New World Library, 1994) 65.

Eckhart Tolle, *A New Earth* (New York/Toronto: A Plume Book, Penguin Group, 2005) 258.

Ira Progoff, *Depth Psychology & Modern Man* (New York: McGraw-Hill Book Company, 1973) 13.

James Hollis, Creating a Life (Toronto: Inner City Books, 2001).

John F. Demartini, *The Breakthrough Experience* (Carlsbad, CA: Hay House, 2002) 40, 41, 44. (3)

Robert M. Doran, *Theology and the Dialectics of History* (Toronto: University of Toronto Press, 1990) 214.

Seneca ... source unknown

Stephen K. Sims, *The Wisdom of Authenticity* (Montreal: self-published, 2015) 69-70.

Wayne Carroll ... personal journal

THEME 16   INWARDNESS

Eckhart Tolle, The Power of Now (Novato, California: New World Library, 1999) 9.

Ira Progoff, *The Symbolic & the Real* (New York: McGraw-Hill Book Company, 1973) 12.

Jalal al-Din Rumi … source unknown

John A. Sanford, *The Kingdom Is Within* (San Francisco: HarperSanFrancisco, 1987) 51.

Joseph Campbell, *The Hero With A Thousand Faces* (Princeton, New Jersey: Princeton University Press, 1972) 77.

M. Esther Harding, *Journey into Self* (New York: Longmans, Green and Co, 1956) 8, 11. (2)

Robert Jingen Gunn, *Journeys into Emptiness* (New Jersey: Paulist Press, 2000) 40.

Sogyal Rinpoche, *The Tibetan Book of Living and Dying* (San Francisco: HarperSanFrancisco, 1994) 51-2.

Teilhard de Chardin, *The Divine Milieu (1957)* 37-8.

Wilson Van Dusen, *The Natural Depth in Man* (1st. edition: New York: Harper & Row, 1972) (2nd. printing: The Swedenborg Foundation, 1981) 71-3.

THEME 17   IMAGINATION

Albert Camus … source unknown

Albert Einstein … source unknown

John Douglas Mullen, *Kierkegaard's Philosophy* (New York: Mentor Book, The New American Library, Inc., 1981) 51, 49. (2)

John O'Donohue, Beauty (New York: Harper Perennial, 2005) 146.

Marilyn Ferguson, *The Aquarian Conspiracy* (Los Angeles: J.P. Tarcher, 1980) 176-7.

Northrop Frye, *The Educated Imagination* (The Massey Lectures – second series – Canadian Broadcasting Corporation, 1963) 60, 57, 66 / 65. (3)

Stephen K. Sims, *River of Awareness* (first edition: Toronto, Novalis Publishing, 2009) 69, 78. (2)

The Bible … Ephesians 3:16, 3:20

THEME 18   MYTH / SYMBOL

Edward F. Edinger, *Ego And Archetype* (New York: Penguin Books, 1972) 117, 130/110, 114, 117. (5)

Gregg Levoy, *Callings* (New York: Three Rivers Press, 1997) 139.

Ira Progoff, *Depth Psychology & Modern Man* (New York: McGraw-Hill Book Company, 1973) 154, 164. (2)

Joseph Campbell, *The Hero With A Thousand Faces* (Princeton, New Jersey: Princeton University Press, 1972) 1, 220-1. (2)

Stephen K. Sims, *River of Awareness* (first edition: Toronto, Novalis Publishing, 2009) 74-5 /*The Wisdom of Authenticity* (Montreal: self-published, 2015) 28-9.

THEME 19   THRESHOLDS

Carl Jung, *Modern Man in Search of a Soul* (New York: A Harvest /HBJ Book, 1933) 99, 108-9. (2)

Daniel J. Levinson, *The Seasons of a Man's Life* (New York: Ballantine Books, 1978) 57-8.

Gregg Levoy, *Callings* (New York: Three Rivers Press, 1997) 147.

Joseph Campbell, *The Power of Myth, with Bill Moyers* (New York: Doubleday, 1988) 11-12, 70, 70.

Joseph Campbell, *The Hero With A Thousand Faces* (Princeton, New Jersey: Princeton University Press, 1972) 6, 8.

Joseph Chilton Pearce, *Magical Child* (New York: Bantam Books, 1980) 18-9.

Rabindranath Tagore, *The Religion of Man* (London: Unwin Books, 1961) 123-4.

THEME 20   HERO PATH

A.D. Sertillanges, *The Intellectual Life* (Netherlands: Bosch Utrecht, 1948) 28.

Bhaskar Goswami ... unpublished writing

Evelyn Underhill, *Mysticism* (New York: Image Books, Doubleday, 1990 / first published 1911) 445.

James Hollis, *Swamplands of the Soul* (Toronto: Inner City Books, 1996) 61-2.

Joseph Campbell, *The Hero With A Thousand Faces* (Princeton, New Jersey: Princeton University Press, 1972) 23, 26. (2)

Joseph Campbell, *Reflections on the Art of Living – A Joseph Campbell Companion* (edited by Diane K. Osbon) (New York: HarperPerennial, 1991) 155. (3)

Rabindranath Tagore, *The Religion of Man* (London: Unwin Books, 1961) 28-9.

Sam Keen, Fire in the Belly (New York, Toronto: Bantam Books, 1992) 153, 156-7. (2)

Stephen K. Sims, *River of Awareness* (first edition: Toronto, Novalis Publishing, 2009) 67.

THEME 21   NOW-PRESENCE

Deepak Chopra, *The Seven Spiritual Laws of Success* (San Rafael, CA: Amber-Allen Publishing and New World Library, 1994) 61.

Eckhart Tolle, The Power of Now (Novato, California: New World Library, 1999) 73.

Jacob Needleman, *Time and the Soul* (San Francisco, Berrett-Koehler Publishers, 2003) 10, 123-4. (2)

John Greenleaf Whittier … source unknown

Kahlil Gibran, *The Prophet* (London: Penguin Group, first published 1926 / Penguin Arkana later edition, 1998) 70.

Pascal Auclair … source unknown

Pema Chodron, *When Things Fall Apart* (Boston: Shambhala Classics, 2000) 144.

Philip Simmons, *Learning to Fall* (New York: bantam Books, 2002) 47-8.

Seneca … source unknown

Thich Nhat Hanh *No Mud, No Lotus* (Berkeley: Parallax Press, 2014) unknown / 68. (2)

THEME 22   SELF-AWARENESS

Anthony de Mello, *The Way To Love* ((New York: Image Books, Doubleday, 1995) 83-4, 77-8, 195-6. (3)

Anthony de Mello, *Walking on Water* (New York: A Crossroad Book, The Crossroad Publishing Company, 2015) 194, 200. (2)

Deepak Chopra, *Ageless Body, Timeless Mind* (New York: Harmony Books. 1993) 36.

Eckhart Tolle, The Power of Now (Novato, California: New World Library, 1999) 14.

Ira Progoff, *The Symbolic & the Real* (New York: McGraw-Hill Book Company, 1973) xv.

Jacob Needleman, *Lost Christianity* (Garden City, New York: Doubleday,1980) 83.

Robert Jingen Gunn, *Journeys into Emptiness* (New Jersey: Paulist Press, 2000) 278-9.

Sebastian Moore, *The Inner Loneliness* (New York: Crossroads, 1982) 10.

Stephen K. Sims, *The Wisdom of Authenticity* (Montreal: self-published, 2015) 134.

Teilhard de Chardin, *Hymn of the Universe* (New York: Collins Fontana Religious Books, 1970) 93.

THEME 23   **ATTENTIVENESS**

Eckhart Tolle, *A New Earth* (New York/Toronto: A Plume Book, Penguin Group, 2005) 116-7.

Eckhart Tolle, The Power of Now (Novato, California: New World Library, 1999) 75.

Evelyn Underhill, *Practical Mysticism* (Columbus, Ohio: Ariel Press,1987 / first published 1914) 65, 69. (2)

Gerald Heard, *Pain, Sex and Time* (Rhinebeck, NY : Monkfish Book Publishing Company, 2004 / first published 1939) 173.

Heather Evans, cited in *The Wisdom of Authenticity* (Montreal: self-published, 2015) 75-6.

Henry Miller ... source unknown

Jalal al-Din Rumi ... source unknown

Lama Surya Das, *Awakening the Buddha Within* (New York: Broadway Books, 1998) 298.

Marilyn Ferguson, *The Aquarian Conspiracy* (Los Angeles: J.P. Tarcher, 1980) 68-9.

R.D. Laing, cited in Connie Zweig & Jeremiah Abrams, *Meeting The Shadow* (New York: Tarcher, Penguin, 1991) xix.

Stephen K. Sims, *The Wisdom of Authenticity* (Montreal: self-published, 2015) 79-80.

THEME 24   QUESTIONS

Bernard Lonergan, *Method in Theology* (Toronto: University of Toronto Press, 1990) 24.

Bernard Lonergan, Insight (Toronto: University of Toronto Press, reprinted 1997) 502.

Deepak Chopra, *Unconditional Life* (New York: Bantam Books, 1992) 11.

Jerome A. Miller, *In the Throe of Wonder*

John Douglas Mullen, *Kierkegaard's Philosophy* (New York: a Mentor Book, The New American Library, Inc., 1981) 3.

Michael Abravanel, cited in *The Wisdom of Authenticity* (Montreal: self-published, 2015) 90-1.

Robert M. Doran, *Theology and the Dialectics of History* (Toronto: University of Toronto Press, 1990) 214.

Sam Keen ... source unknown

Stephen Jenkinson, *Die Wise* (North Atlantic Books, Berkeley, 2015) 118-19.

Stephen K. Sims, *River of Awareness* (first edition: Toronto, Novalis Publishing, 2009) 95, 94. (2)

Stephen K. Sims, *The Wisdom of Authenticity* (Montreal: self-published, 2015) 91-2.

THEME 25   INSIGHT

Alexander Pope ... source unknown

Bernard Lonergan, *Healing and Creating in History* (lecture, 1975) found in the *Third Collection* (Toronto: University of Toronto Press, 2017) 98.

Bernard Lonergan, Insight (Toronto: University of Toronto Press, reprinted 1997) 8.

Bernard Lonergan, *Method in Theology* (Toronto: University of Toronto Press, 1990) 13.

Dalai Lama, *Beyond Dogma* (Berkeley: North Atlantic Books, 1996) 62 / 53. (2)

Ira Progoff, *Depth Psychology & Modern Man* (New York: McGraw-Hill Book Company, 1973) 155.

Lama Surya Das, *Awakening the Buddha Within* (New York: Broadway Books, 1998) 134.

Paulo Coelho ... source unknown

Rabindranath Tagore, *Sadhanna* (Fairfield, IA: 1st. World Library, 2005) 50.

Stephen K. Sims, *River of Awareness* (first edition: Toronto, Novalis Publishing, 2009) 136-7.

Thich Nhat Hanh, *No Mud, No Lotus* (Berkeley: Parallax Press, 2014) 124.

Wilson Van Dusen, The Natural Depth in Man (1st. edition: New York: Harper & Row, 1972) (2nd. printing: The Swedenborg Foundation, 1981) 41.

THEME 26   ACTION

A.D. Sertillanges, *The Intellectual Life* (Netherlands: Bosch Utrecht, 1948) 95-6, 119. (2)

Dalai Lama, *Beyond Dogma* (Berkeley: North Atlantic Books, 1996) 34.

Eckhart Tolle, *A New Earth* (New York/Toronto: A Plume Book, Penguin Group, 2005) 210-11, 294-5. (2)

Mahatma Gandhi, *All Men Are Brothers* (UNESCO, 1958) 174-5.

Mother Teresa, *A Simple Path* (New York: Ballantine Books, 1995 compiled by Lucina Vardey) 138.

Ram Dass, *Grist for the Mill* (Berkeley: Celestial Arts, 1987) 152.

Satish Kumar, *You Are Therefore I Am* (Devon, UK: Green Books Ltd, 2002) 70, 69. (2)

Stephen K. Sims ... personal notes

Thomas R. Kelly, *A Testament of Devotion* (New York: Harper & Row, Publishers, 1941) 89.

Walter E. Conn, *The Desire for Authenticity: Conscience and Moral Conversion* (cited in Vernon Gregson, *The Desires of the Human Heart* (Mahwah, New Jersey: Paulist Press, 1988) 36.

William Butler Yates ... source unknown

THEME 27   REPRESSION

Anthony de Mello, *Walking on Water* (New York: A Crossroad Book, The Crossroad Publishing Company, 2015) 162-3.

ASB@candidcreativity.

Calvin S. Hall & Vernon J. Nordby, *A Primer on Jungian Psychology* (New York: A Mentor Book, 1973) 49.

Carl Jung, *Modern Man in Search of a Soul* (New York: A Harvest /HBJ Book, 1933) 18.

Eckhart Tolle, The Power of Now (Novato, California: New World Library, 1999) 31.

Gerald Heard, *Pain, Sex and Time* (Rhinebeck, New York: Monkfish Book Publishing Co, 2004 /first published 1939) 238.

Robert M. Doran, *Dialogues in Celebration*

Robert M. Doran, *Theology and the Dialectics of History* (Toronto: University of Toronto Press, 1990) 238; 239, 246.

Sebastian Moore, *The Inner Loneliness* (New York: Crossroads, 1982) 51.

Stephen K. Sims, *The Wisdom of Authenticity* (Montreal: self-published, 2015) 84-5.

THEME 28   EMOTIONAL LITERACY

Bernard Lonergan, *Method in Theology* (Toronto: University of Toronto Press, 1990) 33, 32.

Eckhart Tolle, *A New Earth* (New York /Toronto: A Plume Book, Penguin Group, 2005) 136.

Ernest Becker, "*Paranoia*" found in *Angel in Armour* (New York: George Braziller, 1969) 150-1.

Eugene T. Gendlin, *Focusing* (Toronto: Bantam Books /New Age edition, 1978).

Gabor Maté … video lecture

Joe Dispenza … Instagram post, February 22, 2021

Pema Chodron, When Things Fall Apart (Boston: Shambhala Classics, 2000) 69.

Thich Nhat Hanh, *No Mud, No Lotus* (Berkeley: Parallax Press, 2014) 38-39, 101. (2)

Walter E. Conn, *The Desire for Authenticity: Conscience and Moral Conversion* (cited in *The Desires of the Human Heart* (Mahwah, New Jersey: Paulist Press, 1988) 41-2.

THEME 29   AUTHENTICITY

Bernard Lonergan, *Method in Theology* (Toronto: University of Toronto Press, 1990) 52, 110. (2)

Charles Taylor ... source unknown

Dan Berrigan ... source unknown

Jacob Needleman, *The Wisdom of Love* (Sandpoint, ID: Morning Light Press, 2005)) xii-xiii.

John Douglas Mullen, *Kierkegaard's Philosophy* (New York: a Mentor Book, The New American Library, Inc., 1981) 44.

Joseph Campbell, *Reflections on the Art of Living – A Joseph Campbell Companion* (edited by Diane K. Osbon) (New York: Harper-Perennial, 1991) 15.

Mahatma Gandhi ... source unknown

Mooji, *White Fire* (UK: Mooji Media Publications, 2020) 219.

Oscar Wilde ... source unknown

Rabindranath Tagore, *Sadhanna* (Fairfield, IA: 1st. World Library, 2005) 37.

Soren Kierkegaard, quoted by Ernest Becker, *The Denial of Death* (New York: The Free Press, 1973) 82-3.

Stephen K. Sims, *The Wisdom of Authenticity* (Montreal: self-published, 2015) 22.

THEME 30   SELF-KNOWLEDGE

Anthony De Mello, *The Way To Love* ((New York: Image Books, Doubleday, 1995) 193-4.

Carl Jung, *Memories, Dreams, Reflections* (New York: Vintage books, Random House, 1989 – first published 1963) 330-31.

Evelyn Underhill, *Practical Mysticism* (Columbus, Ohio: Ariel Press,1987 / first published 1914) 82, 96. (2)

Friedrich Nietzsche ... source unknown

John Douglas Mullen, *Kierkegaard's Philosophy* (New York: a Mentor Book, The New American Library, Inc. 1981) 4.

Joseph Campbell, *The Hero With A Thousand Faces* (Princeton, New Jersey: Princeton University Press, 1972) 12.

Parker Palmer, *All the Way Down* (Weavings, September / October, 1998) 33-4.

Ram Dass, *Grist for the Mill* (Berkeley: Celestial Arts, 1987) 9.

Satish Kumar, *You Are Therefore I Am* (Devon, UK: Green Books Ltd, 2002) 81.

William Shakespeare, *The Merchant of Venice* (Act 1, Scene 1).